6145

CELEBRATING MARRIAGE

PREPARING THE ROMAN CATHOLIC WEDDING LITURGY

A Workbook for Engaged Couples

Third Edition

PAUL COVINO, Editor
Lawrence Madden, S.J.
Elaine Rendler-McQueeney
John Buscemi

Pastoral Press
Portland • Oregon

Celebrating Marriage: Preparing the Roman Catholic Wedding Liturgy
THIRD EDITION
Paul Covino, Editor
with Lawrence Madden, S.J., Elaine Rendler-McQueeney and John Buscemi

ISBN 978-1-56929-075-0

An imprint of Oregon Catholic Press
5536 NE Hassalo Street
Portland OR 97213–3638
Phone: 1-800-LITURGY (548-8749)
E-mail: liturgy@ocp.org
Web: pastoralpress.com and ocp.org

Printed in the United States of America

Acknowledgments

Designer: John Buscemi

Published with the approval of the Committee on the Liturgy, United States Conference of Catholic Bishops.

Excerpts from the English translation of *Rite of Marriage* ©1969, International Committee on English in the Liturgy, Inc. (ICEL); the English translation of the Psalm Responses and the Lenten Gospel Acclamations from *Lectionary for Mass* ©1969, 1981, 1997, ICEL; excerpts from the English translation of *The Roman Missal* ©1973, ICEL; excerpts from the English translation of *Sacrosanctum Concilium* from *Documents on the Liturgy, 1963–1979: Conciliar, Papal and Curial Texts* ©1982, ICEL; excerpts from the English translation of the *Book of Blessings* ©1988, ICEL. All rights reserved.

Excerpts from the *Lectionary for Mass for Use in the Dioceses of the United States of America, second typical edition* ©2001, 1998, 1997, 1986, 1970 Confraternity of Christian Doctrine, Inc., Washington, D.C. Used with permission. All rights reserved. No portion of this text may be reproduced by any means without permission in writing from the copyright holder.
The English translation of some Psalm responses, some Alleluia and Gospel verses, some Summaries, and the Titles and Conclusion of the Readings, from *Lectionary for Mass* ©1968, 1981, 1997, International Committee on English in the Liturgy, Inc. Washington, D.C. All rights reserved.

Project Editor: Bari Colombari
Publisher: John J. Limb
Director of Editorial Processes: Eric Schumock
Director of Artist Relations & Product Development: Thomas Tomaszek
Editorial Assistance: Rev. Daniel Adams, Glenn CJ Byer, Shawn Freeman, Michael R. Prendergast, Linda Weigel
Book Layout: Tia Regan
Third Edition Cover Design: Le Vu
Art Direction: Gus Torres

TABLE OF CONTENTS

PREFACE

As my own wedding day drew closer, two lists seemed to grow longer with each passing day: the list of things to do before the wedding and the list of people to whom my wife and I owed a great deal of gratitude. The list of people who provided insight and support during the writing and revisions of this book seemed to grow as quickly.

Many colleagues in pastoral ministry and engaged couples offered suggestions and provided a wealth of practical, and oftentimes humorous, reflections on their experience with weddings. I especially want to thank Laura Meagher, Jim Mongelluzzo, Deno and Monica Reed and the members of the Marriage Preparation Teams at Holy Trinity Church in Washington, D.C. who inspired and reviewed much of the material in the original edition of this book. I am also grateful to participants in wedding workshops that I have led and those who reviewed the first two editions or sent in suggestions for this third edition. Their input contributed much to my own understanding and to the changes in this new edition.

Special thanks go to Georgetown University, Holy Trinity Church and the various individuals and foundations which sponsor The Georgetown Center for Liturgy, and, thus, provided the time and resources for writing the original edition of this book. The second edition benefited from the hard work of Barbara Conley Waldmiller and Ken Waldmiller who also contributed great suggestions from their wedding. For this third edition, I am grateful for the contributions of Dan Adams, Leif Kehrwald and Linda Weigel from the Archdiocese of Portland in Oregon, my colleagues in the Office of the College Chaplains at the College of the Holy Cross, and my fellow parishioners on the Liturgy Formation Team at St. Patrick Parish in Whitinsville, Massachusetts, including our pastor, Michael Broderick.

The Pastoral Press endorsed this venture in its infancy, offered patient and encouraging support in the writing and revising, and continues to promote the book to an ever increasing group of churches, chapels, pastoral ministers and engaged couples. My thanks to Dan Connors, Larry Johnson, Virgil Funk, Mary Ellen Cohn,

Kathleen Schaner and Steve Roszel who were involved when Pastoral Press was part of the National Association of Pastoral Musicians, and to Bari Colombari, Michael R. Prendergast, Glenn CJ Byer, Randall DeBruyn, Dave Island, Mary Jo Quinn SCL, Mónica Rada, Tom Tomaszek, Kevin Walsh, Eric Schumock and John Limb at Oregon Catholic Press where Pastoral Press is now located.

Larry Madden, Elaine Rendler-McQueeney and John Buscemi were much more than the authors of their respective chapters. They influenced this entire book, just as they have each been true friends and mentors in the art of pastoral liturgy. I am deeply grateful to each of them.

Finally, I thank and dedicate this third edition to my wife, Anne, and my sons Matthew, Peter, Justin and Benjamin. Their love and encouragement mirror to me each day the divine love that the wedding liturgy celebrates.

Paul Covino

INTRODUCTION

If you are like most engaged couples, you may have discovered by now that the joy, excitement and anticipation that accompanied the announcement of your engagement can quickly give way to anxiety, worry and tension as you prepare for the "big day." You may not have had any ides that getting married required a crash-course in musicians' union regulations, the secrets of reserving a banquet hall within thirty miles of the church, and the most up-to-date principles of excruciatingly correct wedding etiquette!

This workbook has been designed to assist you with something that may have seemed equally veiled in mystery: the preparation of the wedding liturgy. Perhaps you were surprised to learn that you even had a role in this process. Years ago, the bride and groom had very little to say about the wedding liturgy because there was only one way to celebrate a wedding in the Roman Catholic Church. Following the Second Vatican Council (1962–1965), however, the Church issued a revised *Rite of Marriage* which allows several options in the wedding liturgy. This new rite clearly states that the couple is the minister of the sacrament of marriage and should be actively involved in the preparation of the wedding liturgy.

You are not alone in this undertaking. First of all, the priest or deacon who will preside at the wedding liturgy will work with you. In some parishes, a pastoral associate may assist you, while other parishes have a liturgy director, wedding coordinator, marriage preparation team or sponsor couples. Undoubtedly, the parish music minister will be involved. Your parish can give you the names of the people available to help you.

This book is designed to be used as a workbook; feel free to make notes throughout the book, as well as on the planning sheets on pages 121–124. Chapter One provides background information and basic advice, while Chapters Two to Five give the actual texts for the wedding liturgy and information concerning music and environment. You should also be aware that that many parishes and dioceses have specific guidelines relating to the wedding liturgy. Ask the priest, deacon or other pastoral minister working with you about any such guidelines early in the process.

Preparing the wedding liturgy is not difficult; it simply takes time and attention. What is true for shower parties, rehearsal dinners and the wedding reception is equally true for the wedding liturgy: if the basic elements have been prepared well ahead of time, everyone will be less anxious and really free to celebrate. From experience with innumerable weddings, the four writers of this book can attest to the fact that the results will be well worth the effort.

As you prepare the wedding liturgy, you may face some issues that will be similar to situations that you will encounter in married life. For example, many couples are confronted with the question of when and where to seat divorced parents. There may be relatives at the wedding who have not spoken to each other (or to you) in years. Let your approach to these issues now be a positive beginning to the way you will handle similar situations during your marriage. The qualities mentioned in the readings and prayers of the wedding liturgy will serve you well in marriage and in this time of preparation: graciousness, hospitality, generosity, compassion, kindness, peace and love.

Last but not least, set aside time to prepare the wedding liturgy *together*. You may have heard in marriage preparation sessions that communication is vitally important to a healthy marriage; let the process of preparing the wedding liturgy be an opportunity to practice that skill. Discuss the various options in the liturgy with each other, pray over Scripture readings and other texts, talk about the ways in which your families celebrated special events, be sensitive to one another's tastes, and be open to new ways of doing things. With this in mind, preparing the wedding liturgy can bring you closer together and prepare you for married life, and the result will be a celebration that is festive and memorable for all involved.

CHAPTER ONE

AGE-OLD TRADITIONS
AND TIMELY ADVICE

Scene One:

While finalizing plans with the bride for flowers in the church, the florist remarks, "It is customary, you know, to have a white runner rolled down the middle aisle before you enter. It's only plastic, but it is a traditional sign of honor." Uncertain but still smiling, the bride writes another check for seventy-five dollars.

Scene Two:

Noticing the groom's five year old cousin wandering curiously around the tuxedo-clad mannequins, the salesman asks, "Is this young lad the ring bearer? You know, the ring bearer's tux is free with the rental of six or more tuxedos. You are having a ring bearer, aren't you?" Not wanting to hurt his young cousin's feelings, the groom agrees.

Scene Three:

"The Sullivans had the most beautiful soloist for the *'Ave Maria'* at Sally's wedding last month, dear," mother says to daughter. "Who's going to sing it at your wedding?" "Bill and I hadn't planned on having the *'Ave Maria,'* mom,"

VENERABLE TRADITIONS

"Every tradition grows ever more venerable—the more remote is its origin, the more confused that origin is" (Friedrich Nietzsche, *Human, All Too Human,* 1878).

• The custom of having the bridesmaids dress like the bride and the groomsmen like the groom was a way of protecting the bride and groom from evil spirits. If all the women were dressed similarly and all the men were dressed similarly, the evil spirits would not know who the real bride and groom were, and, thus, could not bother the couple.

• The custom whereby the groom is not permitted to see the bride before the wedding dates from a time when most marriages were arranged by the groom and the bride's father. In return for his daughter, the father received money or some other commodity from the groom. Often, the groom did not even meet his bride until the wedding when he made payment to the father. If the groom did not like what he saw, he could call off the wedding, and the father would not receive his payment. To avoid the possibility of such "bad luck," the father did not permit the groom to see the bride until the time of the transaction.

the daughter gingerly responds. Seeing the shock on her mother's face, the bride begrudgingly calls Mrs. Sullivan for the name of the soloist.

Do any of these scenes seem faintly familiar to you? Have you recently discovered, much to your surprise, that several of your relatives and friends are experts on every aspect of a wedding? Have you noticed an increase in the number of times you hear the phrase, "Naturally, you'll want to…," "Of course, you must…," "It is tradition that…," "Etiquette would suggest…," or "We've always done it this way…?" Or are you learning more about the neighbor's daughter's wedding than you ever cared to know? If your answer to any of the above questions is "yes," be assured that you are not alone!

Many of the dos and don'ts one hears about weddings claim to be based on long-standing tradition. There is a popular assumption that weddings have always been celebrated in a certain way and that certain practices are essential for a wedding to be considered "traditional." If these practices are not observed, the wedding is considered "untraditional" or "contemporary." Soon after announcing their engagement, many couples find themselves pressured into opting for one of these two styles.

The truth is that there has been quite an evolution in the understanding of marriage and in the way in which weddings have been celebrated. The history of marriage in the Roman Catholic Church spans two thousand years. It is a rich and diverse heritage, and one that will soon be further enriched by your wedding. Here are just a few highlights to indicate how the current wedding liturgy and some wedding customs developed:

A JOURNEY THROUGH THE TRADITION

• For the first thousand years of the Church's history, there was no specifically Christian rite of marriage. Christians contracted marriage accordingly to the civil and family ceremonies of their culture. Marriage was understood as part of God's plan for humanity. It was also seen culturally as a contract between two families, usually arranged by the groom and the bride's father. As part of the contract, the bride left her family and joined the groom's family. This was expressed ritually by a procession in which the bride was escorted by her father to the groom's home where the father "gave the bride away" to the groom. Using the vows and symbols of their particular culture, the bride promised to be a good wife and mother, and the groom was recognized as the head of this new household.

- In the fourth century, some local churches developed simple marriage blessings for Christian couples, although there was still no Church rite of marriage. After the wedding ceremony, the bishop or priest would visit the couple to congratulate them. The couple, in turn, would ask for his blessing on their marriage. As time passed, parts of the actual wedding ceremony came to be celebrated in the presence of a priest and, eventually, in the church building, constituting the core of the Church's rite of marriage.

- In the early Middle Ages, civil government in much of western Europe was in a state of disarray following a period of political turmoil. In many areas, record keeping and other civic responsibilities fell to the strongest organization remaining in society, the Church, whose clergy and monks were the largest educated group at the time. Thus, Church officials began to exercise jurisdiction over certain aspects of marriage. By the eleventh century, most marriages were fully under Church jurisdiction and were presided over by a priest.

- Prior to the eleventh century, couples were permitted to exchange their marriage vows either in private or in a public ceremony. Since private marriages were occasionally used to force the bride into marriage without her consent, the Church prohibited private marriages in 1215. In that same century, the Church officially identified marriage as a sacrament. These two actions were reaffirmed in 1563 at the Council of Trent (1545–1563) which also added the requirement that Catholics must marry in the presence of a priest and two or three witnesses.

DOWRIES

In ancient times, most marriages were arranged very much like a business deal. Services, property and even people were exchanged in order to gain a marriage partner. Usually, it was the bride who was "purchased" for her value as a household worker and childbearer. The bride's father expected something in return for the loss of his daughter.

In the centuries prior to the birth of Christ, this practice changed in some cultures. While the groom continued to give a gift to the bride's father, he also received goods, land or money along with the bride. This was the bride's dowry, supplied by her father to make her more attractive for marriage.

For more information on dowries and other wedding customs, see *The Wedding Book* by Howard Kirshcenbaum and Rockwell Stensrud (Seabury Press). If you would like to know more about the history of Christian marriages rites, see *To Join Together: the Rite of Marriage* by Kenneth Stevenson (Liturgical Press) and *Documents of the Marriage Liturgy* by Mark Searle and Kenneth Stevenson (Liturgical Press).

THE TRADITION
CONTINUES TO DEVELOP

Like all rituals, the liturgies of the Church continue to develop and change. The *Rite of Marriage* has been a major step in the tradition of Catholic weddings, but it does not mark the end of renewal and reform. Several recent developments show how the tradition is continuing to develop.

• In 1990, the Vatican published a second edition of the Roman Catholic marriage rite, entitled the *Order for Celebrating Marriage.* The English translation and American adaptations of this edition have not yet been finalized. Following approval of the translation and adaptations by the Vatican, this new edition will replace the current *Rite of Marriage.*

• Like the Roman Catholic Church, most Protestant churches have revised their marriage rites in recent years. The revised marriage rites of most of the Christian churches have much in common now, yet another sign that the journey toward unity among the Christian churches is progressing. For information on the marriage rites of a number of Protestant churches, see *The Protestant Wedding Sourcebook* by Sidney Batts (Westminster/John Knox Press).

continued

• The wedding ceremony changed very little in the four centuries following the Council of Trent. Attitudes toward marriage did change, however, especially in the late nineteenth and twentieth centuries. The personal love between a man and a woman came to be recognized as the primary motivation for marriage, replacing contractual arrangements between families. The roles and societal expectations concerning men and women also began to change. The image of the husband as head of the household and the wife as obedient homemaker gave way to a view of the couple as two partners, each possessing talents and rights to a career, yet equally responsible for and involved in creating a home and family.

• In 1963, the Roman Catholic Church began a major reform of all the sacraments at the Second Vatican Council. The Church's understanding of marriage was redefined in light of the contemporary Christian experience of marriage and emerging research in Scripture and sacramental theology. To reflect this new understanding, a revised wedding liturgy, the *Rite of Marriage*, was issued in 1969 and serves as the basis for all weddings in the Roman Catholic Church today, including the marriage a of a Catholic and a non-Catholic.

GETTING BEYOND LABELS

In popular usage, the word "tradition" implies "no change." The surprising lesson from the history of Christian weddings is that change itself is part of the tradition. That is, marriage rites have changed at various times throughout history as the Christian understanding of marriage has developed. What makes the wedding liturgy traditional, then, is not simply the continued use of certain old or popular customs.

Similarly, "contemporary" and "untraditional" are labels often associated with weddings that do not follow an expected pattern or that have elements created by the couples themselves, such as the marriage vows. While the wedding liturgy does allow for a variety of options, it also has a given structure and provides formulas for the vows and other texts. Its celebration is governed by the liturgical guidelines of the Church. A wedding is contemporary, therefore, not because of its originality or rejection of established patterns.

"Traditional" and "contemporary," as used in popular language, simply imply a particular style. When describing church liturgies, however, they refer not to distinct styles, but to two inseparable characteristics that are always present. The word "traditional" comes from the Latin word for "hand down." Your wedding liturgy will be traditional because it is based on the *Rite of Marriage* and, therefore, hands down the Christian faith concerning marriage. It will be contemporary because, as it is celebrated, the wedding liturgy will reveal your love for and commitment to one another and make present here and now God's love for you in its actions and symbols. In other words, the wedding liturgy is both traditional and contemporary by its very nature.

So, what does this say about the task you are now facing —the preparation of your wedding liturgy? It says what this task is *not*:

> **Preparing the wedding liturgy is not a matter of creating a ceremony according to a particular style.**

This does not mean that your wedding will not have a style of its own. It just means that style is not the primary consideration in preparing the wedding liturgy. There are more basic things to consider first.

This simple point may well be the most challenging one for couples today. Why? To put it bluntly, weddings are big business. From florists to professional wedding consultants, there is substantial pressure on couples to "go all out" in setting a style for the wedding. By now, you have probably discovered how expensive that can be. At the same, you may be discovering that the more important and substantial aspects of the wedding can easily get overlooked in the rush to have everything "just so."

continued

PARTICIPATION IS PRIMARY

It doesn't have to be that way with your preparations for the wedding liturgy. Let this rule guide you and serve as a general job description:

The goal of your preparation is to encourage the full and active participation of all who will gather to celebrate your marriage. This is best accomplished by carefully preparing and celebrating the central features of the wedding liturgy. The primary focus of your attention, then, is the *Rite of Marriage,* in which the structure and individual elements of the wedding liturgy are presented. These are basic and essential to the wedding liturgy.

Nothing is more vital to liturgy than the active participation of all the worshippers. This is a fundamental principle of Roman Catholic liturgy, grounded in the teachings of the Second Vatican Council. Like all liturgies, a wedding is a participatory event, not just an event to be watched. You are inviting family and friends to witness your exchange of vows and to celebrate with you, not to be spectators at a show. This distinction is fundamental and makes a world of difference in the wedding liturgy. It *is* possible to draw everyone — Catholics and non-Catholics, churchgoers and non-churchgoers — into the celebration of your marriage. It just requires some attention to the basic elements of the wedding liturgy. This is not difficult, but it will demand more of you than simple stylistic considerations.

SIX PIECES OF BASIC ADVICE

The remainder of the book will discuss the individual elements of the wedding liturgy. As an introduction to that, here are six pieces of basic advice to make your preparation as effective as possible.

ONE: Distinguish between what is essential and what is not.

As you review the wedding liturgy in Chapter Two, you may note that some of the practices that you may be accustomed to seeing at weddings are not listed. These are instances of popular practices which, although commonly used at weddings, are not actually part of the wedding liturgy. They usually fall into three categories: social customs, forms of personal expression and religious devotions. Each of these can enhance a wedding liturgy or detract from it. It's all a matter of distinguishing them from what is essential and keeping them in perspective.

Social Customs. Couples often experience a great deal of pressure to shape their wedding according to others' expectations. This pressure is usually strongest when social customs are involved. These customs are not necessarily religious, nor do they necessarily reflect contemporary attitudes toward marriage. They are simply "expected social behavior."

Wearing special gowns and tuxedos and having bridesmaids, flower girls, ring bearers and white aisle runners are all examples of social customs. Other examples are the practice whereby the bride is "given away" by her father, and the practice of seating the relatives and friends of the groom on one side of the aisle and those of the bride on the other side. Some social customs are actually based in superstition, such as the practice whereby the groom is not allowed to see the bride before the wedding. The church does not require any of these customs and, in fact, many couples have abandoned them in favor of more meaningful options suggested in the *Rite of Marriage*.

Forms of Personal Expression. Your wedding is obviously a deeply personal event, and it is natural to want to personalize the wedding liturgy. The *Rite of Marriage* allows for this by providing many options. You may select, for example, the prayers and Scripture readings from a number of possibilities. You will work with the parish musicians on the selection of music for the wedding. You may be involved in selecting flowers and other elements for the environment inside the church. All of these will reflect your faith and values.

A WEDDING IS
PUBLIC BUSINESS

The following is from an essay that appeared in TIME magazine in 1983:

The vows that couples devise are, with some exceptions, never as moving to the guests as they are to the couple. Too often the phrases, words overblown and intimate and yearning all at once, go floating plumply around the altar, pink dreams of the ineffable. Friends and family lean forward in their pews. The clergy-person beams inscrutably, abetting the thing, but keeping counsel. The guests are both fascinated and faintly appalled to be privy to such intense and theatrical whisperings. John Lennon and Yoko Ono once held press conferences while lying in bed, and the effect of the self-made vows is sometimes obscurely the same…If the bride and groom have intimacies to whisper, there are private places for that. A wedding is public business.[1]

Contrary to popular opinion, "public" is not necessarily the opposite of "personal," and "personal" is not necessarily the same as "private." When the author of the essay portrayed the wedding as "public business," he was not denying its personal nature.

continued

There are other forms of personal expression that go beyond the options provided in the wedding liturgy. For example, you may have a special song, poem or story that reflects your love for one another. Because of its importance in your relationship, you may want to share it with your relatives and friends at the wedding. The meaning that it holds for you, however, may be very difficult to convey to others, especially within the brief time of the wedding liturgy when so much else is happening. Such elements might be more effective within some other part of the wedding celebration. For example, the special song could be featured at the wedding reception or the poem could be read as part of a blessing or prayer before the rehearsal dinner.

Religious Devotions. The wedding liturgy is rich in religious symbolism, and the various readings and prayers provide a broad perspective on the Christian experience of marriage. As you review the options in Chapters Two to Five, your own religious faith will influence and be reflected in the choices you make.

As a further expression of their religious faith, some couples include in the ceremony religious devotions that are not actually part of the wedding liturgy. At some weddings, the bride places flowers before a statue of Mary. Another example is the lighting of a "unity" or "marriage" candle from two smaller candles, representing the union of the bride and groom. These practices can be meaningful if they actually reflect an important element of the couple's faith. As with forms of personal expression, the question to ask here is whether this meaning can be conveyed effectively to others within the wedding liturgy. It can be just as, if not more, effective to feature such devotions at other parts of the celebration where they can add a healthy religious dimension. For example, the rehearsal could begin with a prayer and the placing of flowers before a statue of Mary, while the lighting of a marriage candle could be part of a blessing or prayer before the meal at the reception.

TWO: Give priority in your preparation and in the celebration to the essentials.

Let's take a look at what is already in place in the wedding liturgy before your preparations even begin, that is, the essentials: a gathering of people, an opening and closing procession, two or three Scripture readings, a homily, prayer of the faithful (intercessions), the blessing and exchange of rings, the vows and a variety of related prayers. When the wedding takes place within Mass, all the regular elements of a Sunday Eucharist are also involved. Usually, a fair amount of music is included. In other words, quite a bit takes place within a single liturgy, usually lasting no more than an hour.

In liturgy, it is more effective to do a few things well than to try to do many things. Quality is more important than quantity. Put your energy, then, into reviewing and making the most of the options already contained in the *Rite of Marriage*. Before considering any additions to the wedding liturgy, make sure that the essential elements listed above have been prepared well and remember that additions will not make up for a weak celebration of the essentials.

Finally, ask the following questions of any practices that you consider adding to the wedding liturgy:

Does it add something that is not already in the liturgy?

Does it reflect a Christian understanding of marriage?

Does it reflect your faith and values, or is it simply something you saw done at a friend's wedding?

Does it encourage the participation of those who will gather to celebrate your marriage, or does it render them merely spectators?

In summary, will it help to highlight, rather than obscure, the basic elements of the wedding liturgy?

THREE: Plan the wedding day as a whole, with the liturgy as its centerpiece.

At some weddings, the events that come before and after the liturgy are fun and full of human warmth, while the liturgy itself is stilted, cold and out of character with the rest of the day. People breathe a sigh of relief when the socially

A Wedding Is Public Business
continued

He was stating that it is not a private affair. Twenty years before the essay appeared, the Second Vatican Council presented a similar sentiment: "Liturgical services pertain to the whole Body of the Church."[2]

To say that "a wedding is public business" is not only to acknowledge the presence of others in the church; it implies preparing the wedding in such a way as to encourage their active participation in it. This principle is a helpful guide to determine whether some social customs, form of expression or religious devotion that you are considering adding to the wedding liturgy will be effective.

[1] Lance Morrow, "The Hazards of Homemade Vows," TIME, June 27, 1983, p. 78.

[2] *Constitution on the Sacred Liturgy*, 26. More on this quote in "Your Wedding: A Celebration for the Whole Church" in Chapter Two.

enforced rigidity of the ceremony is over and they can move on to the "real celebration" — the reception.

Yes, the wedding liturgy is a different kind of event than the reception; it has a form and spirit that are unique. When prepared and celebrated well, though, the wedding liturgy can be the high point of the day, an event of even more human warmth than the reception. The essential ingredient to make this happen is hospitality, the deliberate and conscious effort to welcome and pay attention to the people who will gather to celebrate your marriage.

FOUR: Do not underestimate the power of the non-verbal elements of the wedding liturgy.

The wedding liturgy is more than a series of prayers, readings and verbal commentary. It is a ritual act made up of significant symbols, gestures and texts. The music, the environment of the church building, the manner in which people are greeted, the way that processions move, the printed order of celebration or program given to people for the liturgy, the placement of the couple and other worshippers: all of these will "speak" as loudly as will the prayers, readings and other texts of the liturgy. When carefully prepared, these non-verbal elements complement the verbal ones; ignored or poorly prepared and celebrated, they can negate even the most beautiful of texts.

FIVE: Take advantage of the people who will be preparing the wedding liturgy with you.

In the Introduction, we said that you are not alone in the preparation of the wedding liturgy. This is both reassurance and advice: reassurance that others will work with you and advice to take advantage of them.

First of all, both the bride and the groom are involved in the preparation. This is not "her special day" any more than it is "his special day." It is a special day for the couple and the Church. This is evident in the *Rite of Marriage* which consistently emphasizes the unity of the bride and groom in all aspects of the wedding, as well as the role of the Church.

Those who will work with you include the priest or deacon who will preside at the liturgy and the parish music minister. Depending on your parish, a liturgy coordinator, pastoral associate, wedding coordinator, marriage preparation team or sponsor couple may also be available to assist you. These people bring a great deal of experience to the job. Share your ideas with them and be open to their advice.

SIX: Don't wait until the last minute to prepare the wedding liturgy!

Can you imagine planning the wedding reception on one week's notice? In the same way, give yourselves — and others —plenty of time to prepare the wedding liturgy. Talk, discuss, review the options and make the necessary arrangements well in advance. The wedding rehearsal is just what the name implies: a rehearsal of what has already been decided. It is not the time to make decisions about liturgical and musical options. If the preparations have been done well in advance, there is no reason why the rehearsal needs to be any longer than thirty minutes. Let the priest, deacon, wedding coordinator or someone else from the parish run the rehearsal. Get through the rehearsal efficiently and then go enjoy the company of family and friends!

The next four chapters will present the four major areas for your consideration: the wedding liturgy, the readings, the music and the environment. A work sheet is provided on pages 121–124 for you to indicate your planning decisions as you go through these chapters.

CHAPTER TWO

THE CEREMONY:
THE WEDDING LITURGY

O nce you have decided to celebrate your marriage in the Roman Catholic Church, the first step is to contact your parish. This should not be delayed since many parishes now require a minimum of several months between this initial contact with the parish and the wedding date. During these months, you will probably be asked to participate in a parish or diocesan marriage preparation process. This is also the time to begin the preparation for your wedding liturgy.

The first two issues in your wedding liturgy preparations are very basic: the place and the date.

PLACE

When marriage was viewed as primarily a family affair, the family home was the appropriate and ordinary place for the wedding celebration. As the marriage of Christians came to be seen in the larger context of the Church, the ordinary place for the wedding celebration became the parish Church.

Liturgical services are not private functions but are celebrations of the Church which is "the sacrament of unity"… Liturgical services pertain to the whole Body of the Church. They manifest it and have effects upon it. But they also touch individual members of the Church in different ways, depending on their orders, their role in the liturgical services, and their actual participation in them… Rites which are meant to be celebrated in common, with the faithful present and actively participating, should, as far as possible, be celebrated in that way rather than by an individual and quasi-privately.[1]

This statement from the Second Vatican Council presents one of the most basic characteristics of Christian liturgy: its communal nature. All liturgy takes place in the context of a particular parish community within the context of the universal Church.

While the wedding liturgy will touch you, your family and friends in an especially intimate way, it pertains to the local parish and to the larger Church as well. When you exchange your vows, you offer a

continued

14

This remains true today. (See "Your Wedding: A Celebration for the Whole Church," left.)

The wedding liturgy is celebrated in the parish church of the bride or the groom. There is no longer a preference for the bride's parish over the groom's parish. The important thing is to celebrate your wedding in the parish where one or both of you are members. Often, it is required that you be registered as parishioners before the wedding can be scheduled. This is a formal acknowledgment that you are members of the parish in which the wedding will be celebrated.

DATE AND TIME

In general, a wedding liturgy may be celebrated on any day of the year. There are various considerations, though, that make certain days and times more appropriate than others.

The parish schedule. Parishes often have a fixed schedule of times for weddings based on the availability of the church, the priest or deacon and the musicians. Other parish activities may also restrict certain dates and times. In some places, weddings are not scheduled on Sundays because of the regular Mass schedule. In other places, weddings are occasionally celebrated at Sunday Masses. Ask the priest, deacon or wedding coordinator about your parish schedule.

Special seasons. Lent is a season of penance in preparation for Easter, while Advent looks ahead to Christmas and to Christ's second coming at the end of time. The tone of the Church's worship during these times is more subdued. This may be reflected quite visibly in the church environment during Advent and Lent (see Chapter Five). While weddings are not prohibited during these times, other times of the year are more appropriate for the festive nature of the wedding liturgy. The Easter Triduum (Holy Thursday evening through Easter Sunday) is the high point of the Church's year, and sacraments other than baptism, confirmation and the Eucharist are usually not celebrated during this time. On certain days, the prayers and readings of that day, rather than those from the *Rite of Marriage,* would be used if a wedding were celebrated. These days include the Sundays of Advent,

Lent and Easter, major occasions known as solemnities, the eight days beginning with Easter Sunday (the Octave of Easter), All Souls' Day (November 2), Ash Wednesday and Holy Week. The dates for some of these days and seasons vary from year to year, so check with your parish for this year's dates.

One last piece of advice concerning the date and time of your wedding can save you a lot of unnecessary trouble:

> **Make sure you have reserved the date and time of your wedding with the parish before reserving the reception facilities or printing the invitations.**

THE PEOPLE IN YOUR WEDDING LITURGY

Next, we turn our attention to the people who will play a part in the celebration of the wedding liturgy. As you know from Sunday Mass, there are various roles within the liturgy. These roles are defined as "ministries" and the people who fulfill them as "ministers."

The Assembly

As at any liturgy, the fundamental ministry within the wedding liturgy is that of the assembly of people who gather to celebrate. Everyone in the church for your wedding is, first and foremost, a member of this assembly—the two of you, the wedding party, the priest or deacon, and the musicians included. The assembly celebrates the liturgy; individual members of this assembly fulfill various special ministries within the liturgy.

You may have been to weddings where this point was more or less overlooked, with the result that the majority of people at the wedding were treated like an audience at a show. When this happens, people refrain from participating in the liturgy, and the whole experience can end up being about as engaging as watching someone else's home movies! Recall our general job description from Chapter One:

visible sign of God's presence and love to the parish in which your wedding is celebrated. You create a new family within that community. At the same time, the Church and, in particular, the local parish promises to be there for you in times of need. You are making a commitment to each other and to the Church. In turn, the Church is making a commitment to you.

The guidelines which many parishes and dioceses have established for weddings reflect this commitment. The Church's concern is expressed before the wedding in its encouragement to you to take part in a marriage preparation process. This concern continues in the assistance and guidance the parish offers for your wedding liturgy. As a liturgy of the parish, your wedding will be influenced and shaped by the parish's typical patterns of worship, especially its celebration of Sunday Mass. Look upon these guidelines not as obstacles to be overcome, but rather as an expression of the Church's desire to celebrate your wedding as an integral and welcome part of the parish's worship life.

[1] *Constitution on the Sacred Liturgy,* 26–27.

WHEN A CATHOLIC MARRIES SOMEONE WHO IS NOT CATHOLIC

Years ago, it was not unusual for a non-Catholic who was engaged to a Catholic to "convert" to Catholicism prior to the wedding. Often this was done to avoid any conflict that a difference of religions may have presented to the marriage and to the upbringing of children.

Today the situation is somewhat different. While the number of marriages between Catholics and non-Catholic has increased over the last few decades, more and more of these couples have decided to maintain their different religious affiliations. The Catholic Church's own policy for receiving new members (*The Rite of Christian Initiation of Adults* and the *Reception into Full Communion with the Catholic Church*) is sensitive to this concern and cautions against joining the Church only because of an upcoming marriage to a Catholic.

When a Catholic marries a non-Catholic, the Church's concerns is that the Catholic be able to remain active in his or her faith and that, as far as possible, any children be brought up as Catholics. According to the requirements of your diocese, the priest or deacon may have to write to the local bishop to apply for one of the following:

continued

The goal of your preparation is to encourage the full and active participation of all who will gather to celebrate your marriage.

Since the wedding liturgy is a parish celebration, it is preferable that parishioners, as well as family and friends from outside the parish, be part of the assembly. To encourage this, some parishes announce weddings in the parish bulletin with an invitation for parishioners to participate in the liturgy. In other places, weddings are occasionally celebrated within regularly scheduled Sunday and Saturday evening Masses so that the community may be present.

The Couple

The two of you are the ministers of the sacrament of marriage in the Roman Catholic wedding liturgy. You give yourselves to one another in marriage. The priest or deacon serves as the Church's official witness, but he does not "pronounce you man and wife."

Since a great deal of attention is focused on you during the wedding, you also set the tone for the assembly by your own attitudes and behavior. If, for example, you are at ease before the liturgy and taking the time to greet people as they arrive, people will feel welcome and relaxed. If you enter into the prayers and singing during the liturgy, others in the assembly will be inclined to follow your lead.

Although permitted, it is not recommended that you take on additional ministries during the liturgy, such as reader or extraordinary minister of holy Communion. These other ministries are best fulfilled by others in the assembly. The roles mentioned in the previous two paragraphs will require most of your energy and attention if they are to be done well.

The Presiding Minister

The minister who leads the celebration of the wedding liturgy is referred to as the presiding minister. When the wedding is celebrated within Mass, a priest will preside at the wedding liturgy. When the wedding is celebrated outside of Mass, a priest or deacon may preside. The *Order for Celebrating*

Marriage, published by the Vatican in 1990, provides for a trained layperson to preside at a wedding outside of Mass, but this option has not been approved for use in the United States yet. Usually, a priest or deacon from the parish presides since the wedding is seen as a parish celebration. Priests or deacons from outside the parish may preside at weddings with the delegation of the local pastor. If the priest or deacon is from out of state, he may be required to obtain a civil license from the state in which the wedding will take place to officiate at the wedding.

Inviting additional priests to "concelebrate" at a wedding is permitted but not highly recommended. The presence of additional priests in the sanctuary tends to visibly detract from your central role as ministers of the sacrament of marriage. If another priest is coming to the wedding, you could ask him to lead a blessing at the rehearsal dinner, reception or some other part of the wedding festivities.

As marriages between Catholics and people from other religious traditions become increasingly common, it is not unusual for the couple to request that a minister from the other religious tradition be involved in the wedding liturgy. This minister may, for example, lead one of the prayers or blessings. Certain parts of the wedding liturgy, such as questions concerning the consent and exchange of vows, are reserved to the Catholic priest or deacon, however. Speak with the priest or deacon before extending an invitation to another minister, and discuss the logistics of who will do and say what well in advance of the rehearsal. If planned and carried out well, this can be a beautiful and significant sign of the ecumenical or interfaith dimension of your marriage. (See "When a Catholic Marries Someone Who Is Not Catholic," left.)

The Witnesses

Every member of the assembly at your wedding is a witness to your exchange of vows. At the same time, three particular witnesses have a special role to play in the liturgy and for Church records. First, the Church's "official witness" is the priest or deacon who asks for and receives your consent. He does this by asking you the three questions in the statement of intentions and by receiving your consent in the exchange of vows (see pages 34–35). The other two witnesses stand by you during the marriage rite. They need not be Catholic or even baptized; their primary duty is to attest to the fact that the marriage took place. While it is customary to have one male ("the best man") and one female ("the maid/matron of honor"), it is possible to have two males or two females.

Ushers and Bridesmaids

There is no more effective way to show people how much you appreciate their presence at your wedding and to encourage their participation than through hospitality. The members of your wedding party can be of tremendous help here. Ask them to greet people cordially as they arrive at the church, to give them the printed order of celebration for the wedding, and to lead them to a seat near other worshippers. The men and women in your wedding party can assist with this form of hospitality. There is no reason to limit the role to men.

Musicians

The music at your wedding has the power to encourage or stifle the participation of the assembly. The norm in the Roman Catholic liturgy is participatory music; that is, the majority of music during the liturgy should be sung by the entire assembly. A cantor, or leader of song, can significantly enhance the assembly's participation in the liturgy by reviewing music that may be unfamiliar before the liturgy and by providing subtle direction during the liturgy. The spirit and enthusiasm that the assembly's participation in the singing will bring to your wedding liturgy will be well worth the relatively small expense of hiring a leader of song.

What other musicians are involved in the wedding will depend on the specific musical choices that you work out with the parish music minister. The various possibilities are discussed in Chapter Four.

Readers (Lectors)

In some places, parishioners who read at Sunday Mass also fulfill this role at weddings. These readers have experience in reading in that particular church, they will be at ease in this role at the wedding, and they know the logistics of things such as how to work with the microphone. If this is not the practice in your parish, you will want to select readers from among the people who will be at the wedding. People who serve as readers in their home parishes are good choices because of their familiarity with the role. Otherwise, look for people who are good public speakers. More on this in Chapter Three.

Extraordinary Ministers of Holy Communion
(Weddings within Mass only)

Extraordinary ministers of holy Communion—or Communion ministers, as they are commonly known—assist the priest with the distribution of Communion. As with readers, extraordinary ministers of holy Communion from the parish are the logical first choice since they are experienced and familiar with the procedures. Otherwise, think of people who will be at your wedding who are extraordinary ministers of holy Communion in their home parishes. Finally, with the permission of the parish priest, members of the assembly who are not commissioned as extraordinary ministers of holy Communion may be asked to serve in this role for this special event. In this case, ask them to attend the rehearsal in order to learn what they will be doing at the wedding.

Altar Servers

Altar servers assist the presiding minister in a number of ways during the liturgy. Some parishes automatically schedule them for weddings; others do not use them for weddings at all. Inquire about the local practice, or if you wish to ask a relative or friend who is an altar server at another parish to serve at your wedding. In this case, it would be wise to ask the altar server to attend the rehearsal. If a person has never been an altar server, it is best not to ask him or her to serve in this role at the wedding liturgy.

HOW MANY EXTRAORDINARY MINISTERS OF HOLY COMMUNION WILL WE NEED?

The presiding priest always distributes the eucharistic elements at Mass. To determine the number of additional extraordinary ministers of holy Communion that will be needed for your wedding, try to estimate how many people will be receiving Communion. A good rule of thumb is one person to distribute the Eucharistic Bread and two to administer the cup for every 50 to 75 people who will be receiving Communion. If you estimate, for example, that about 60 people will be receiving Communion, then plan on two extraordinary ministers of holy Communion in addition to the priest. For 130 people, plan on five extraordinary ministers of holy Communion in addition to the priest.

This formula is somewhat general. The parish may have its own suggestions for how many extraordinary ministers of holy Communion are needed based on past experience.

WHEN A CATHOLIC MARRIES A JEW

When American Jews marry today, more than half of them marry people who are not Jewish. This is a matter of great concern to the Jewish community which harbors a legitimate fear for the survival of the Jewish people and their religion. But if a Catholic and a Jew have decided to marry, the wedding liturgy can be a spiritually nourishing event and can do much to bring the two families to a deeper understanding of each other's traditions and spiritualities. Catholic-Jewish marriages can work and work very well, but there are special difficulties that need to be faced. The couple may wish both a rabbi and a priest to participate in their wedding; this is possible although it can be quite difficult to find a rabbi who will participate in such an interfaith, or mixed marriage. If local rabbinic help is unavailable, consult the Dovetail Institute for Interfaith Family Resources (775 Simon Greenwell Lane, Boston, KY 40107, 800-530-1596, dovetailinstitute.org).

Frequently the Jewish party in a Catholic-Jewish wedding does not feel comfortable being married in a Catholic church, so a dispensation from canonical form may be sought by the Catholic priest or deacon

continued

20

PHOTOGRAPHS AND VIDEO RECORDINGS

Photographs and video recordings serve as an attractive reminder of your wedding, but you don't want the picture taking or video recording to interfere with the event. Through the use of various lenses, film speeds and digital technologies, a professional photographer or video recorder need not be right up front in order to get good pictures. He or she can be positioned discreetly to the side and back of the church. Ask the photographer or video recorder in advance to keep his or her movements around the church to a minimum during the liturgy. Most parishes also allow a period of time before or after the liturgy for formal posing of pictures, and many parishes have written guidelines for photographers and video recorders.

A bigger challenge might be to keep the amateur photographers and video recorders among your family and friends under control during the liturgy. People standing up to take pictures not only distract from what is going on, but they also block the vision of those seated behind them. Perhaps a politely worded note could be included in the order of celebration asking people to refrain from snapping pictures, or at least from using flash photography, until after the liturgy.

PRINTED ORDER OF CELEBRATION

A well designed printed order of celebration— also known as a worship aid or program — can greatly enhance the assembly's participation in the liturgy. The order of celebration is distributed by the ushers or bridesmaids as people arrive at the church, and it should include the music that the assembly will be invited to sing and an outline of the liturgy. The parish music minister can provide you with most of the information for the order of celebration. He or she may also have samples for you to look over from previous weddings at the parish. More details about the order of celebration and two samples are provided on pages 105–116.

THREE FORMS OF THE WEDDING LITURGY

The *Rite of Marriage* provides three forms for celebrating marriage in the Roman Catholic Church:

I **The Rite of Marriage During Mass** is normally used when two Catholics marry.

II **The Rite of Marriage Outside Mass** is used when a Catholic marries a baptized person from another Christian church.

III **The Rite of Marriage Between a Catholic and an Unbaptized Person** is used when a Catholic marries someone who is not Christian.

In the first form, the wedding is situated in the context of a Mass. In the second and third forms, Mass is not celebrated. Each of the forms is equally valid in the eyes of the Church; a wedding is not any more or less complete because of the celebration of Mass.

There is some flexibility in which form may be used. For example, it is possible to use the Rite of Marriage During Mass when a Catholic marries a non-Catholic, but it is not encouraged since current Church regulations essentially limit the reception of Communion at Mass to Catholics. In this case, the celebration of Mass may serve as a source of disunity as a time when you want to stress unity. There are also times when the Rite of Marriage Outside Mass may be celebrated when two Catholics marry, such as when a priest is not available and a deacon will be presiding at the wedding liturgy. The second form may also be the more honest choice if, for example, you are both Catholic but do not participate in Mass on a regular basis. The choice of which form you will use should be made in consultation with the priest, deacon or other pastoral minister.

The prayers and readings used in each of the three forms are, generally, the same. The exchange of vows and rings takes place after the homily in all three forms. All three forms also have the same basic structure:

When a Catholic Marries a Jew
continued

(see 'When a Catholic Marries Someone Who is Not Catholic," pages 16–17). This means that the wedding may take place somewhere other than a church with a rabbi acting as the principal officiant and yet the marriage will also be registered in the Catholic Church. In such a ceremony, with the agreement of the rabbi, the priest may lead certain parts of the wedding such as a reading from the New Testament (1 Corinthians 12:31—13:8a is usually acceptable) followed by a brief homily. He could also join the rabbi in the Aaronic blessing, which the rabbi could say in Hebrew and the priest in English. These and other options should be worked out with the rabbi and priest well in advance of the wedding.

—Lawrence Madden, S.J.

BRINGING THE FORMS TO LIFE

Take a look at one of your cookbooks. (You must have received at least one at showers by now!) Do you see how recipes are usually set up? First, there's a list of the ingredients in the order they are mixed in. Then, there's a description of the actions (chop, fry, etc.) needed to bring these ingredients to life as a cake, pie or *fettucine alfredo.*

The outline of the three forms of the wedding liturgy on these pages is similar to the list of ingredients in a recipe. It's simply a list of what happens when. To prepare the wedding liturgy effectively, it's also necessary to know what energies are needed to bring these elements to life.

Sulpician Father Eugene Walsh (1911–1989), a pioneer in liturgical renewal, offered a concise summary of these energies. What he said about Sunday Mass is equally applicable to the wedding liturgy:

> All members of the assembly… have three things to do at Sunday liturgy: They gather; they listen; they respond. All assembly members, without exception, must invest personally in each of these sacramental actions, or Sunday liturgy loses its power to give life. The deliberate presence

continued

THE INTRODUCTORY RITES
THE LITURGY OF THE WORD
THE MARRIAGE RITE
(THE LITURGY OF THE EUCHARIST)
THE CONCLUDING RITES

Here is the outline of each of the three forms:

I. RITE OF CELEBRATING MARRIAGE DURING MASS

THE INTRODUCTORY RITES
Gathering of the Assembly
Procession
Greeting
Penitential Rite
Gloria
Opening Prayer

THE LITURGY OF THE WORD
Old Testament Reading
Responsorial Psalm
New Testament Reading
Gospel Acclamation
Gospel
Homily

THE MARRIAGE RITE
Address and Statement of Intentions
Consent and Exchange of Vows
Blessing and Exchange of Rings
Prayer of the Faithful

THE LITURGY OF THE EUCHARIST
Preparation of the Gifts
Eucharistic Prayer
The Lord's Prayer
Nuptial Blessing
Sign of Peace
Breaking of the Bread
Communion
Prayer after Communion

THE CONCLUDING RITES
Blessing
Dismissal
Recessional

II. RITE OF CELEBRATING MARRIAGE OUTSIDE MASS

THE INTRODUCTORY RITES
Gathering of the Assembly
Procession
Greeting
Opening Prayer

THE LITURGY OF THE WORD
Old Testament Reading
Responsorial Psalm
New Testament Reading
Gospel Acclamation
Gospel
Homily

THE MARRIAGE RITE
Address and Statement of Intentions
Consent and Exchange of Vows
Blessing and Exchange of Rings
Prayer of the Faithful
Nuptial Blessing

THE CONCLUDING RITES
The Lord's Prayer
Blessing
Recessional

III. RITE OF CELEBRATING MARRIAGE BETWEEN A CATHOLIC AND AN UNBAPTIZED PERSON

THE INTRODUCTORY RITES
Gathering of the Assembly
Procession
Rite of Welcome

of assembly members through these sacramental actions makes Sunday liturgy rise above the level of deadly routine and mechanical ritual.[1]

The introductory rites of the liturgy are designed to transform the many individuals in the church into a unified assembly of worshippers, ready to celebrate and hear the Scriptures.

During the Liturgy of the Word, the energy involved is listening, both to the Scriptures and to the homily.

In the marriage rite, you respond to the Scripture readings in your exchange of vows. The assembly responds as the witnesses to this sacrament, pledging their support to you. When marriage is celebrated within Mass, the energy of responding continues in the eucharistic prayer and in Communion.

Finally the response to God's word continues in daily life each time we attend to the needs of others. The two of you carry on this response each day of married life as your love develops and a new Christian family is established.

[1] *Giving Life: Ministry of the Parish Sunday Assembly* (Portland OR: OCP Publications, 1993), Assembly Ed. 9871, p. 21.

NEW LIFE FOR
AN OLD CUSTOM

More and more couples are becoming involved in the hospitality extended to guests arriving for the wedding celebration. Here is a wonderful story from a couple who greeted their arriving guests personally while building in some quiet time before the wedding for that special moment when they saw one another in their wedding clothing for the first time.

"As we began preparations for our wedding, we realized one of the most important elements we wanted to stress was hospitality. Friends and family are important to each of us and we wanted to convey that message as well as we possibly could. We wanted to make our guests feel welcome at the 'biggest day of our lives,' and one of the best ways we felt we could do that was for both of us to be at the front doors of the church greeting people as they came to the wedding.

"Months before the wedding, upon hearing the rumor of this 'untraditional' beginning, relatives and friends tried desperately to help us 'see the error of our ways— before it was too late!' When confronted with comments like 'You can't do that; it's bad luck,' 'What will your aunts say?' and 'It's simply not done,' we recalled some of the background of popular wedding customs that we had read in the "Venerable Traditions" sidebar of

continued

THE LITURGY OF THE WORD
 Old Testament Reading
 Responsorial Psalm
 New Testament Reading
 Gospel Acclamation
 Gospel
 Homily

THE MARRIAGE RITE
 Address and Statement of Intentions
 Consent and Exchange of Vows
 Blessing and Exchange of Rings
 Prayer of the Faithful
 Nuptial Blessing

THE CONCLUDING RITES
 The Lord's Prayer
 Blessing
 Recessional

STEP BY STEP THROUGH
THE WEDDING LITURGY

Once you have identified which of the three forms of the wedding liturgy you will be using, the next step is to review each of the individual elements of the liturgy. Note those place where there are options and discuss which option you prefer, indicating your choices on the planning sheet on pages 121–124. Phrases in some of the prayers are in parentheses. These phrases may be omitted if appropriate. You will also see the letter "*N.*" in a number of the prayers. This simply indicates where your name(s) would be inserted in the prayer.

THE INTRODUCTORY RITES

Gathering of the Assembly

Take a look at the list of people who will be at your wedding: relatives of the bride, relatives of the groom, friends and associates from work and school, people from different parts of the country or from other countries, Catholics from other parishes, Catholics who are not regular church-goers, people from other religious traditions who may be unfamiliar with the Catholic liturgy or even uncomfortable in a Catholic Church. At the wedding, these various people—many of whom may not know one another—will come together to witness and celebrate your marriage.

People are generally more at ease and open to celebrate when they know the people around them. At weddings, this often does not happen until sometime during the reception. People come into the church as strangers and leave as strangers, so it's no wonder they are reticent in joining in the liturgy. Some very simple things can be done as people arrive at the church to make them feel welcome and to gather them into an assembly that is ready to celebrate the liturgy together. For this reason, the time before the entrance procession is the primary opportunity to set a positive tone for the wedding. Consider the following ways to take advantage of this opportunity:

(a) To borrow a line from the musical *My Fair Lady,* "Get me to the church on time!" In fact, plan on arriving about one half hour before the time of the wedding. Give yourselves time to relax at the church and, in fairness to others, start the wedding on time.

(b) By all means, get dressed at home. Some parishes do provide a room for changing, but fussing over gowns and tuxedos that soon before the wedding usually only adds to the anxiety and increases the blood pressure. For the sake of a few wrinkles, it's not worth it.

(c) Make sure that people are warmly greeted as they arrive at the church, preferably by the two of you and your parents. This is probably the single most effective thing you can do to make people feel welcome, to thank them for joining in this special celebration, and to encourage their participation in the liturgy. This also allows you to introduce friends and relatives *before* the liturgy, rather than waiting until the reception. Such interaction in church is not irreverent; it serves to shape a worshipping assembly out of the many individuals who will be at your wedding. (See "New Life for an Old Custom," left.)

New Life for an Old Custom
continued

Celebrating Marriage. Then we asked a simple question of each of our naysayers: 'Would you invite people to your home for a meal and not greet them at the door?' The resounding answer was, 'Of course not!' We explained that we felt the same principle applied to the wedding. We saw one of our primary roles as host and hostess and it would simply be inhospitable not to greet people who came to celebrate with us.

"Then came the dilemma: what about that first time he sees her in her bridal gown and she sees him 'dressed to the nines?' We talked a lot about that moment. We wanted it to be a very special time for the two of us. In the 'traditional' option, only the groom is seen before the wedding and the bride is secluded away in a dimly lit, uncomfortable room separated from all the festivities. The first time he sees her and vice versa is a very powerful, intimate moment shared with 250 other people! We wanted to find a way to share that moment with each other. Our solution was to have Ken pick Barb up on the way to church.

"When Ken arrived at the house, Barb went to a room in a quiet part of the house. Ken went to the room and opened the door. The moment was very powerful for each of us. He looked so handsome and she radiated with happiness. We stared at each other for a few moments, frozen partly because the magnitude of the step we were taking was finally sinking in and partly because we were nervous, excited and speechless all at once! To be able to have this time alone with each other and not have to share it with anyone else for a while

continued

was precious to us. As we rejoined the rest of the people in the house, we were met with raves of joy and tears of happiness. The photographer, who was at the house too, was able to get some great pictures that he otherwise would have missed.

"Arriving at the church, we both went to the front doors and greeted each person who arrived for our wedding. We were having so much fun seeing friends and family, we weren't as nervous as we expected we might be, and the whole atmosphere of the church was festive. Our witnesses and parents were also at the door and they had a great time; neither mother cried as much as we feared because they were too busy having fun!

"By beginning our wedding celebration this way, we also eliminated another 'traditional' trap: the receiving line. The idea of standing for well over an hour making little more than small talk with people who were important to us and who had come to celebrate with us while the rest of our guests began the reception festivities without us, went against the sense of hospitality we had tried to impart for our wedding liturgy. Without the receiving line, we were able to enjoy the reception with everyone else. We were able to take advantage of that extra time and spend more time with our guests.

"So, with a little bit of planning and ingenuity, we were able to begin our married life symbolizing the graciousness and hospitality that we hope to emulate throughout the rest of our lives together."

—Barb Conley Waldmiller
and Ken Waldmiller
Married June 23, 1990
St. Michael Church, Syracuse, NY

(d) Avoid prelude music that is overpowering or somber. Pleasant, upbeat music in the church as people arrive contributes to effective gathering. (See Chapter Four for specific suggestions.)

(e) Seat people close together and toward the front of the church. While the first one or two rows are often reserved for the immediate family and the wedding party, the other front rows should be filled as people arrive. Fill one row before seating people in the next. If the church has seating on various sides of the altar, seat people in the front rows on the various sides. There is also no reason to have a "bride's side" and a "groom's side" in the church. The aim is to encourage people to interact and form a cohesive assembly, not to separate them into different contingents. Ushers, bridesmaids and other people can assist in seating people; this role is not limited to males.

(f) Just before the entrance procession, the leader of song could briefly rehearse music that might be unfamiliar as a way to encourage people to sing during the liturgy.

Procession

The entrance procession at a wedding is an extended form of the regular entrance of the priest and other ministers at Sunday Mass. The *Rite of Marriage* describes the procession in this way: "…the ministers go first, followed by the priest, and then the bride and bridegroom. According to local custom, they may be escorted by at least their parents and the two witnesses" (20). Adaptations may be made to this format, such as the inclusion of ushers and bridesmaids in addition to the two witnesses ("best man" and "maid/matron of honor") in the procession lineup. The procession may also be simplified so that the two of you enter alone in procession and meet the priest at the front of the aisle.

The *Rite of Marriage* does not mention the form of procession in which the bride enters, accompanied by the bridesmaids and her father, and meets the groom at the front of the aisle. This form developed at a time when a wedding literally signified the transfer of the bride between two men: from father to husband (see "Venerable Traditions," page 2). Many couples—certainly many women—would not see their wedding in this light today. The procession, as envisioned in the *Rite of Marriage,* is the ritual entrance of the ministers for the liturgy. Since the two of you together are the ministers of the sacrament of marriage, you are both included in the procession. This also reflects the Church's understanding that the bride and groom are equal and complementary partners in marriage.

There is no reason to limit parental involvement in the procession to the bride's father. Each of your parents has contributed to your formation leading up to this day. By including the parents of the bride and the groom, the procession reflects the reality that a new family is being created from two existing families. You are not displacing the bride's father but rather honoring the unique role that each of your parents has played in your life.

The procession may be led by an altar server or another minister carrying the processional cross, followed by a reader carrying the *Book of the Gospels*, the priest or deacon, ushers and bridesmaids, the best man and the maid/matron of honor, the groom escorted by his parents and the bride escorted by her parents. If a minister from another religious tradition is involved, he or she could walk next to or in front of the priest or deacon. The two of you could also walk in together at the end of the procession, with your parents in front of you. Once the procession has reached the front of the aisle, you could each kiss your parents. Then, all go to their respective places. (See Chapter Five for specific suggestions about seating arrangements for the couple, witnesses, immediate family, ushers and bridesmaids.)

Greeting

Once everyone is in place and the music has ended, the presiding minister leads the Sign of the Cross, the traditional beginning of Christian prayer:

LINING UP THE PROCESSION

There are several ways to organize the entrance procession at a wedding. Here are three possible arrangements:

Model A
    altar server carrying
       processional cross
    reader carrying the *Book of*
       the Gospels
    priest or deacon
    usher and bridesmaid
    usher and bridesmaid
    best man and maid/matron
       of honor
    groom with his parents
    bride with her parents

Model B
    altar server carrying
       processional cross
    reader carrying the *Book of*
       the Gospels
    priest or deacon
    bridesmaid
    usher and bridesmaid
    best man and maid/matron
       of honor
    groom's parents
    bride's parents
    bride and groom

Model C
    altar server carrying
       processional cross
    reader carrying the *Book of*
       the Gospels
    priest or deacon
    usher and bridesmaid
    usher and bridesmaid
    best man and maid/matron
       of honor
    groom's parents
    groom
    bride's parents
    bride

BEGINNING WITH HOSPITALITY

The introductory rites of the liturgy are designed to gather people into a unified assembly that is ready to hear the Word of God. Hospitality is a key ingredient in making this happen. Consider this adaptation from Elaine Rendler-McQueeney to emphasize a spirit of hospitality at the beginning of your wedding liturgy:

After the Sign of the Cross and presiding minister's greeting, the presiding minister or the couple addresses the assembly, inviting them to greet each other. The following words could be used:

Presiding Minister: **Today we come together to celebrate a feast of great joy and unity. Two families become one larger family. Two individual lives become a shared life. Let us turn to each other and welcome our families and friends.**

or

Couple: **Today we come together to celebrate one of the happiest days of our lives. We are grateful to all of you who have come from near and far to be with us today and to witness our marriage. So that we might rejoice, pray and sing together as one family, please introduce yourselves to those around you.**

continued

Presiding
Minister: **In the name of the Father, and of the Son, and of the Holy Spirit.**

All respond: **Amen.**

He then greets all present with one of the following greetings:

1. **The grace of our Lord Jesus Christ and the love of God and the fellowship of the Holy Spirit be with you all.**

2. **The grace and peace of God our Father and the Lord Jesus Christ be with you.**

3. **The Lord be with you.**

The response in each case is: **And also with you.** (This response may be changed to **And with your spirit** as additional revisions are introduced into the Catholic liturgy.) Although not mentioned in the *Rite of Marriage,* it would be appropriate for you, as ministers of the sacrament, to greet people briefly in your own words after the presider's greeting. If you plan to do this, ask the priest or deacon if a microphone could be placed near where you will be standing. After the greeting(s), a hymn could be sung by the entire assembly. Known as a "gathering song," this is an effective opportunity for the assembly to join their voices in prayer at the beginning of the liturgy. (See Chapter Four for suggestions.)

Penitential Rite
(Weddings within Mass only)

In the penitential rite, we praise God for continually showing us mercy. In keeping with the nature of the wedding liturgy, this rite is kept very simple. (In the revised *Order for Celebrating Marriage,* the penitential rite is omitted altogether.) The priest begins with these or similar words: **My brothers and sisters, to prepare ourselves to celebrate the sacred mysteries, let us call to mind our sins.** Then, one of the following is used:

1. All say the following:

I confess to almighty God,
and to you, my brothers and sisters,
that I have sinned through my own fault
in my thoughts and in my words,
in what I have done,
and in what I have failed to do;
and I ask blessed Mary, ever virgin,
all the angels and saints,
and you, my brothers and sisters,
to pray for me to the Lord our God.

<table>
<tr><td>2.</td><td>Priest:</td><td>Lord, we have sinned against you:
Lord, have mercy.</td></tr>
<tr><td></td><td>All:</td><td>Lord, have mercy.</td></tr>
<tr><td></td><td>Priest:</td><td>Lord, show us mercy and love.</td></tr>
<tr><td></td><td>All:</td><td>And grant us your salvation.</td></tr>
</table>

3. Various texts may be used with the third form of the penitential rite. The following is an example of texts that would be appropriate for a wedding:

<table>
<tr><td>Priest:</td><td>You showed us the power of God's love
through your obedient death on the cross:
Lord, have mercy.</td></tr>
<tr><td>All:</td><td>Lord, have mercy.</td></tr>
<tr><td>Priest:</td><td>You reveal your love for the Church
in the union of husband and wife:
Christ, have mercy.</td></tr>
<tr><td>All:</td><td>Christ, have mercy.</td></tr>
<tr><td>Priest:</td><td>You call us to love one another
as you have loved us:
Lord, have mercy.</td></tr>
<tr><td>All:</td><td>Lord, have mercy.</td></tr>
</table>

In each case, the priest then says:

**May almighty God have mercy on us,
forgive us our sins,
and bring us to everlasting life.**

At the conclusion of this welcome, the presiding minister or leader of song might use these or similar words to address the guests:

Let us continue our celebration by singing praise to God with our gathering song "Joyful, Joyful, We Adore Thee" (or whatever song you have chosen).

This extra moment of welcome and invitation as part of the introductory rites will not only put the guests at ease, but will fulfill our call as Christians to welcome the stranger. This moment can be particularly effective if people who are not Catholic are present or if there are people who are coming to this church for the first time. Experience has proven that people will join in the singing and response more heartily if they have been acknowledged and welcomed and invited to participate.

All respond: **Amen.** If option 1 or 2 was used, the following invocations conclude the penitential rite:

Priest: **Lord, have mercy.**
All: **Lord, have mercy.**

Priest: **Christ, have mercy.**
All: **Christ, have mercy.**

Priest: **Lord, have mercy.**
All: **Lord, have mercy.**

Gloria
(Weddings within Mass only)

If the wedding takes place on a Sunday outside of Advent or Lent or on a solemnity (that is, a major Church feast day), the Gloria is the next prayer of the wedding liturgy. Otherwise, it is not used. (The text of the Gloria may be changed as additional revisions are introduced into the Catholic liturgy.)

**Glory to God in the highest
  and peace to his people on earth.
Lord God, heavenly King,
almighty God and Father,
  we worship you, we give you thanks,
  we praise you for your glory.
Lord Jesus Christ, only Son of the Father,
Lord God, Lamb of God,
you take away the sin of the world:
  have mercy on us;
you are seated at the right hand of the Father:
  receive our prayer.
For you alone are the Holy One,
you alone are the Lord,
you alone are the Most High
  Jesus Christ,
  with the Holy Spirit,
  in the glory of God the Father. Amen.**

Opening Prayer

The presider then says **Let us pray,** pauses for all to pray silently for a few moments, and then says one of the following options for the opening prayer:

1. Father,
    you have made the bond of marriage
    a holy mystery,
    a symbol of Christ's love for his Church.
    Hear our prayers for *N.* and *N.*
    With faith in you and in each other
    they pledge their love today.
    May their lives always bear witness
    to the reality of that love.

    We ask this through our Lord Jesus Christ,
        your Son,
    who loves and reigns with you and the Holy Spirit,
    one God, for ever and ever.

2. Father,
    hear our prayers for *N.* and *N.,*
    who today are united in marriage before your altar.
    Give them your blessing,
    and strengthen their love for each other.

    We ask this through our Lord Jesus Christ,
        your Son,
    who lives and reigns with you and the Holy Spirit,
    one God, for ever and ever.

3. Almighty God,
    hear our prayers for *N.* and *N.,*
    who have come here today
    to be united in the sacrament of marriage.
    Increase their faith in you and in each other,
    and through them bless your Church
        (with Christian children).

    We ask this through our Lord Jesus Christ,
        your Son,
    who lives and reigns with you and the Holy Spirit,
    one God, for ever and ever.

4. Father
   when you created mankind
   you willed that man and wife should be one.
   Bind *N.* and *N.*
   in the loving union of marriage;
   and make their love fruitful
   so that they may be living witnesses
   to your divine love in the world.

   We ask this through our Lord Jesus Christ,
       your Son,
   who lives and reigns with you and the Holy Spirit,
   one God, for ever and ever.

The response in each case is: **Amen.**

THE LITURGY OF THE WORD

The focus of this section of the wedding liturgy is the proclamation of God's Word in the Scripture readings. Since this is discussed in detail in other chapters, it will not be repeated here. Chapter Three provides the options for the Old Testament reading, the New Testament reading and the Gospel, as well as commentary on each. The Responsorial Psalm and Gospel acclamation are intended to be sung; they are discussed in Chapter Four.

The homily is delivered by a priest or deacon, normally the presiding minister. It addresses the sacramental nature of Christian marriage as exemplified in the readings that have just been proclaimed and in your own lives. If the priest or deacon does not know you very well, he may try to find out more about you in your meetings with him before the wedding. In this way, he can personalize the homily.

THE MARRIAGE RITE

The marriage rite is the central part of the wedding liturgy. Through the prayers and actions of this rite, you give yourselves to one another in marriage freely and unconditionally in the presence of the Church's witnesses: the priest or deacon, the best man and maid/matron of honor, and the entire assembly. Consider the following ways to enhance the power of this rite:

(a) Stand in such a way that you can face each other and allow the assembly to see you, with the best man and maid/matron of honor standing to either side of you. The priest or deacon stands facing you, either at the head of the aisle or slightly forward and to the side of where you are standing so that he does not obstruct the assembly's view of you. The assembly should remain seated so that all might be able to have a clear line of vision. (See Chapter Five for suggested arrangements.)

(b) Have a microphone placed in front of you so that all might hear what is being said. This is, after all, the high point of liturgy and all the witnesses—assembly included—should be able to hear it.

(c) Don't allow additional elements to overwhelm the essential prayers and symbolic actions in this rite. Although brief, the marriage rite has a richness in its texts and actions. Put your energy into proclaiming your vows and the prayer for the exchange of rings clearly. Pay attention to placing the rings on one another's fingers graciously and visibly. Consider singing a brief acclamation after the exchange of vows and after the exchange or rings.

Address and Statement of Intentions

Once the priest or deacon, the best man and maid/matron of honor, and the two of you are in place, the priest or deacon addresses you in these or similar words:

My dear friends, you have come together in this church so that the Lord may seal and strengthen your love in the presence of the Church's minister and this community. In this way you will be strengthened to keep mutual and lasting faith with each other and to carry out the other duties of marriage. And so, in the presence of the Church, I ask you to state your intentions.

He then asks you the following questions:

N. and *N.*, **have you come here freely and without reservation to give yourselves to each other in marriage?**

You each respond: **We have.**

Will you love and honor each other as man and wife for the rest of your lives?

You each respond: **We will.**

(Will you accept children lovingly from God, and bring them up according to the law of Christ and his Church?

You each respond: **We will.)**

Consent and Exchange of Vows

The priest or deacon then says: **Since it is your intention to enter into marriage, join your right hands, and declare your consent before God and his Church.** You join your right hands and declare your consent (that is, exchange your vows) using one of the following formulas:

1. **I, *N.*, take you, *N.*, to be my wife/husband. I promise to be true to you in good times and in bad, in sickness and in health. I will love you and honor you all the days of my life.**

2. **I, *N.*, take you, *N.*, for my lawful wife/husband, to have and to hold, from this day forward, for better, for worse, for richer, for poorer, in sickness and in health, until death do us part.**

You may also use one of the following formulas in which the priest or deacon poses the question and you each answer, **I do.**

3. *N.*, **do you take *N.* to be your wife/husband? Do you promise to be true to her/him in good times and in bad, in sickness and in health, to love her/him and to honor her/him all the days of your life?... I do.**

4. *N.*, **do you take *N.* for your lawful wife/husband, to have and to hold, from this day forward, for better, for worse, for richer, for poorer, in sickness and in health, until death do you part?... I do.**

The first two formulas represent a more powerful declaration of your consent, since you address one another directly. Memorizing the formula is not difficult, and it allows you to look at each other as you exchange your vows. If you are nervous about forgetting the formula, write it down on an index card and hold the card as you say the vows. An altar server or the priest or deacon could also hold a copy of the vows for you.

After you have declared your consent, the priest or deacon says:

You have declared your consent before the Church. May the Lord in his goodness strengthen your consent and fill you both with his blessings. What God has joined, men must not divide.

All respond: **Amen.**

In some parishes, the assembly joins in singing a brief musical acclamation after the exchange of vows (see "Acclamations in the Marriage Rite," right).

Blessings and Exchange of Rings

The priest or deacon then blesses the rings using one of these prayers:

1. **May the Lord bless † these rings
which you give to each other
as the sign of your love and fidelity.**

2. **Lord, bless these rings which we bless † in your name.
Grant that those who wear them
may always have a deep faith in each other.
May they do your will
and always live together
in peace, good will and love.
We ask this through Christ our Lord.**

3. **Lord,
bless † and consecrate *N.* and *N.*
in their love for each other.
May these rings be a symbol**

ACCLAMATIONS IN THE MARRIAGE RITE

Occasionally couples request that a song be sung after the exchange of vows and rings. Often, this ends up being a solo performance that does not invite the assembly's participation. A more effective way to incorporate music in the marriage rite is through simple acclamations that the assembly is invited to sing after your exchange of vows and again after the exchange of rings. Such an acclamation serves to praise God for the commitment that you have just undertaken. It also provides a way for your family and friends to express their support and affirmation of your commitment.

The revision of the wedding liturgy that was published by the Vatican in 1990 suggests this type of musical acclamation after the exchange of vows. It also suggests an acclamation or a hymn of praise after the exchange of rings. While these revisions have not yet been promulgated in the Church in the United States, such musical acclamations have already been used quite effectively in weddings throughout the country. See Chapter Four and the two sample programs at the end of this book for more information on these acclamations.

of true faith in each other,
and always remind them of their love.
We ask this through Christ our Lord.

The response in each case is **Amen.** The best man or maid/matron of honor may hold the rings for the blessing. As he says the blessing prayer, the priest or deacon makes the sign of the cross (†) over the rings. He may also sprinkle the rings with blessed water. Then, the groom places the bride's ring on her finger, and the bride places the groom's ring on his finger. As you each do this, you say the following:

N., **take this ring as a sign of my love and fidelity. In the name of the Father, and of the Son, and of the Holy Spirit.**

After you have exchanged the rings, the assembly could join in singing a brief musical acclamation, or the priest or deacon may invite the assembly to applaud as a joyful sign of their approval of the marriage. If the two of you wish to exchange a kiss at this point, by all means do so.

Prayer of the Faithful

The marriage rite concludes with the prayer of the faithful, also knows as the general intercessions. This is a set of prayers specifically directed to the larger needs of the world, the Church and our communities. Usually, the priest, deacon, or other members of the parish write these prayers for Sunday Mass. For the wedding liturgy, you may want to write them or, at least, suggest specific intentions to be included in the prayers. This is a good opportunity to personalize the liturgy, while remembering the needs of others in the midst of the day's joy.

For example, you might want to pray for deceased or sick relatives, friends and relatives who could not be at the wedding, parents, godparents and others who have been influential in your lives, and parish and school communities of which you have been a part. These should be balanced with broader concerns such as the poor, homeless and unemployed of the city where the wedding is taking place, Church and government officials, and peace among nations. If there are going to be people from Protestant or Orthodox Churches at the wedding, you might want to include a prayer for the unity of Christian Churches. In the same way, you could include a prayer for Jews, Muslims and members of other religious traditions if they will be represented in the assembly.

The prayer of the faithful begins with a brief introduction by the priest or deacon. Then, the intentions are announced by a reader. This may be one of the people who read the first or second reading, or it may be someone else. There are ordinarily five or six intentions, each simple and relatively brief. Following each intention, the reader says **Let us pray to the Lord** or **We pray to the Lord,** to which the assembly responds with an invocation such as **Lord, hear our prayer.** After the last intention, the priest or deacon says a concluding prayer which sums up and completes the prayer of the faithful.

The priest, deacon, or other pastoral minister can assist you with the composition of these prayers. Two samples are also provided on pages 119–120.

(If your wedding will be celebrated outside of Mass, the prayer of the faithful is followed by the nuptial blessing. Turn to page 43.)

THE LITURGY OF THE EUCHARIST
(Weddings within Mass only)

The Liturgy of the Eucharist at a wedding is celebrated in the same way as it is at Sunday Mass with one exception: the addition of the nuptial blessing before Communion. There are also options for the prayers of this part of the liturgy that are specifically related to marriage.

Preparation of the Gifts

After the prayer of the faithful, the assembly is seated and the bread and wine for the Eucharist are brought to altar by two people from the assembly. Ideally, you want to choose people who are not fulfilling other special roles such as usher or reader. For example, godparents or other significant people

WEDDING GIFTS

Wedding gifts are a very concrete way for people to express their congratulations and best wishes to you as you begin your marriage. Whether it is a unique crystal bowl or the third toaster you've received, each gift is a symbol of the people who gave it and of their love and concern for you. Long after the wedding day, the gifts remind you of these people and help you to recapture the joy of the day.

Gifts also play an important part in the Liturgy of the Eucharist. At Sunday Mass, three gifts are brought forward: bread, wine and a collection of money. The bread and wine become the basic elements of the eucharistic meal, while the money supports the parish's activities, particularly outreach to those in need. Each of these gifts represents the members of the assembly and their participation in the Eucharist and the social mission of the Church, the two mutual dimensions of the Christian life.

Because of the importance of gifts in weddings and in the liturgy, two suggestions are offered for your consideration as you prepare the wedding liturgy:

(1) Friends and relatives are often exceedingly generous at weddings. You may already be overwhelmed by

continued

the outpouring of gifts. Some couples have found equally generous ways to respond to this outpouring of gifts by making a gift of their own to the needy.

- If you have received the infamous duplicate toasters, why not donate one to a local soup kitchen or shelter for the homeless?

- If you have received money, perhaps you could make a donation to the parish's social outreach committee or food bank.

- In some places, the couple provides a large basket of food that is brought forward at the preparation of gifts. After the wedding, a member of the parish delivers the basket to a needy family.

- On their wedding invitations, some couples ask guests to bring a non-perishable food item to the wedding for the local food pantry. Baskets to collect the food could be set up in the church vestibule.

- Online charitable wedding registries allow couples to designate a charity to which they request that guests donate in lieu of a wedding gift. Examples of such registries are JustGive.org, IDoFoundation.org and whatgoesaround.org.

Gifts such as these serve the same function as the collection of money at Sunday Mass. They provide an opportunity to share the joy of your wedding with those who are in need.

continued

in your lives who are otherwise not serving in a special liturgical ministry at the wedding might be delighted to be asked to do this. They simply walk to the place where the bread and wine have been set out before Mass, pick up the vessels containing the bread and wine, and walk in a simple procession to the altar, where they hand the bread and wine to the priest. Then, they return to their seats. Those carrying the gifts may bow to the altar, as a sign of reverence, if it is local custom.

The priest receives the bread and wine and says a silent prayer of blessing. Then, he says a prayer over the gifts using one of the following.

1. **Lord,
   accept our offerings
   for this newly-married couple, *N.* and *N.*
   By your love and providence you have
       brought them together;
   now bless them all the days of their
       married life.
   We ask this through Christ our Lord.**

2. **Lord,
   accept the gifts we offer you
   on this happy day.
   In your fatherly love
   watch over and protect *N.* and *N.*,
   whom you have united in marriage.
   We ask this through Christ our Lord.**

3. **Lord,
   hear our prayers
   and accept the gifts we offer for *N.* and *N.*
   Today you have made them one in the
       sacrament of marriage.
   May the mystery of Christ's unselfish love,
   which we celebrate in this Eucharist,
   increase their love for you and for each other.
   We ask this through Christ our Lord.**

The response in each case is: **Amen.**

All stand and the priest begins the eucharistic prayer, which is the central prayer of the Mass. In it, we thank God, recount the story of Jesus' Last Supper and invoke God's Spirit on the bread and wine and on us. The prayer is led by the priest and the assembly sings acclamations at three points in the prayer. The following dialogue opens the prayer:

Priest: **The Lord be with you.**

All: **And also with you.**

Priest: **Lift up your hearts.**

All: **We lift them up to the Lord.**

Priest: **Let us give thanks to the Lord our God.**

All: **It is right to give him thanks and praise.**

The eucharistic prayer continues as the priest says one of the following Prefaces:

1. **Father, all-powerful and ever-living God,**
   we do well always and everywhere to give
   you thanks.
   By this sacrament your grace unites man and woman
   in an unbreakable bond of love and peace.
   You have designed the chaste love of
   husband and wife
   for the increase both of the human family
   and of your own family born in baptism.

   You are the loving Father of the world of nature;
   you are the loving Father of the new
   creation of grace.
   In Christian marriage you bring together
   the two orders of creation:
   nature's gift of children enriches the world
   and your grace enriches also your Church.

   Through Christ the choirs of angels
   and all the saints
   praise and worship your glory.
   May our voices blend with theirs
   as we join in their unending hymn:

(2) In the early centuries of Christianity, people brought bread and wine for Mass from their homes. The wedding liturgy offers a marvelous opportunity to renew this ancient custom. You or a member of your family could provide a bottle of wine for the Eucharist. Perhaps one of your relatives is a good cook and is anxious to do something to help with the wedding preparations. Why not ask that person to bake bread? Here is a recipe that is consistent with current Church regulations for the bread used at Mass:

Ingredients:
$2\frac{1}{2}$ cups of flour
$\frac{1}{2}$ cup unbleached white flour
$1\frac{1}{4}$ cups lukewarm water (110° F.)

• Preheat oven to 350° F.

• Mix all the ingredients together in a bowl until all the flour is gathered together. Place on the counter and knead for about 5 to 6 minutes. The dough will be on the stiff side, so there is not a great need for very much extra flour to facilitate kneading. Kneading is most important to prevent puffing or ballooning.

• When the dough is smooth and pliable, after kneading, form dough into a ball and let rest for about 5 minutes, covered with a dampened cloth, to prevent a crust from forming.

• Divide the dough in half, and roll each half to an eight inch diameter and about $\frac{1}{4}$ inch thick.

continued

• Lightly grease a cookie sheet. Bake the bread immediately upon completion of rolling out. Bake for about 16 or 17 minutes. The bread should not brown, so the color will remain pretty much the same but will lighten somewhat. It must not be overbaked, as some moisture is needed to retain the proper texture.

• Cool and wrap in plastic or foil and freeze until a few hours before using.

This recipe produces two 8-inch round loaves, which is enough bread for about one hundred people at Communion. Do not break the loaves into smaller pieces as this will be done by the priest during the Liturgy of the Eucharist.

2. Father, all-powerful and ever-living God,
we do well always and everywhere to give
you thanks
through Jesus Christ our Lord.

Through him you entered into a new
covenant with your people.
You restored man to grace in the saving
mystery of redemption.
You gave him a share in the divine life
through his union with Christ.
You made him an heir of Christ's eternal glory.
This outpouring of love in the new covenant of grace
is symbolized in the marriage covenant
that seals the love of husband and wife
and reflects your divine plan of love.

And so, with the angels and all the saints
in heaven
we proclaim your glory
and join in their unending hymn of praise:

3. Father, all-powerful and ever-living God,
we do well always and everywhere to give you thanks.

You created man in love to share your divine life.
We see his high destiny in the love of
husband and wife,
which bears the imprint of your own divine love.

Love is man's origin,
love is his constant calling,
love is his fulfillment in heaven.

The love of man and woman
is made holy in the sacrament of marriage,
and becomes the mirror of your everlasting love.

Through Christ the choirs of angels
and all the saints
praise and worship your glory.
May our voices blend with theirs
as we join in their unending hymn:

After the Preface, all join in the first of the three acclamations in the eucharistic prayer. These acclamations are usually sung (see Chapter Four). This first acclamation is called the "Sanctus" (from the Latin word for "holy").

Holy, holy, holy Lord, God of power and might,
heaven and earth are full of your glory.
  Hosanna in the highest.
Blessed is he who comes in the name of the Lord.
Hosanna in the highest.

After the "Sanctus" acclamation, the assembly kneels during the rest of the eucharistic prayer which the priest proclaims. There are several optional texts for the rest of the eucharistic prayer, each of them too lengthy to reprint here. If you would like to see a copy of these prayers and perhaps make a suggestion about which one will be used at the wedding, ask the priest in one of your preparatory meetings with him.

In the middle of the eucharistic prayer, the priest sings or says: **Let us proclaim the mystery of faith.** The assembly responds by singing the memorial acclamation. There are four options for this acclamation:

A. **Christ has died,**
   Christ is risen,
   Christ will come again.

B. **Dying you destroyed our death,**
   rising you restored our life.
   Lord Jesus, come in glory.

C. **When we eat this bread and drink this cup,**
   we proclaim your death, Lord Jesus,
   until you come in glory.

D. **Lord, by your cross and resurrection**
   you have set us free.
   You are the Savoir of the world.

The eucharistic prayer ends with the following:

Priest: **Through him,**
        with him,
        in him,
        in the unity of the Holy Spirit,

all glory and honor is yours,
almighty Father,
for ever and ever.

The assembly responds by singing the final acclamation: **Amen.**

The Lord's Prayer

The Lord's Prayer, or "Our Father," is the most basic Christian prayer. Especially in the wedding liturgy, it serves a most important function by uniting worshippers from various Christian Churches in a common prayer. It is introduced by the priest or deacon.

Presiding
Minister: **Let us pray with confidence to the Father in the words our Savior gave us:**

All: **Our Father, who art in heaven,
hallowed be thy name;
thy kingdom come;
thy will be done on earth as it is in heaven.
Give us this day our daily bread;
and forgive us our trespasses
as we forgive those who trespass against us;
and lead us not into temptation,
but deliver us from evil.**

The prayer that normally follows the Lord's Prayer in the Mass ("Deliver us, Lord, from every evil…") is omitted in the wedding liturgy. Although not mentioned in the *Rite of Marriage,* it would be appropriate, as well as a sign of hospitality and respect, to conclude the Lord's Prayer instead with the traditional ecumenical ending, or "doxology," if there are going to be Christians from other Churches at the wedding:

All: **…deliver us from evil.
For thine is the kingdom, and the
power, and the glory,
for ever and ever. Amen.**

Nuptial Blessing

There are two blessings of the couple in the wedding liturgy: the nuptial blessing and the final blessing. When the wedding is celebrated within Mass (form I), the nuptial blessing follows the Lord's Prayer. When the wedding is celebrated outside of Mass (form II or III), the nuptial blessing follows the prayer of the faithful, and the Lord's Prayer then follows the nuptial blessing.

The priest or deacon faces the couple and prays one of the following options for the nuptial blessing:

1. **My dear friends, let us turn to the Lord and pray**
   that he will bless with his grace this woman (or *N.*)
   now married in Christ to this man (or *N.*)
   and that (through the sacrament of the
       body and blood of Christ,)
   he will unite in love the couple he has
       joined in this holy bond.

   Father, by your power, you have made
       everything out of nothing.
   In the beginning you created the universe
   and made mankind in your own likeness.
   You gave man the constant help of woman
   so that man and woman should no longer
       be two, but one flesh,
   and you teach us that what you have united
   may never be divided.

   Father, you have made the union of man and woman so
       holy a mystery that it symbolizes the marriage
       of Christ and his Church.

   Father, by your plan man and woman are united,
   and married life has been established
   as the one blessing that was not forfeited
       by original sin
   or washed away in the flood.

   Look with love upon this woman, your daughter,
   now joined to her husband in marriage.
   She asks your blessing.
   Give her the grace of love and peace.

Note:

In option #1 for the nuptial blessing, "through the sacrament of the body and blood of Christ" is omitted when the wedding is celebrated outside of Mass. Two of the three following paragraphs may also be omitted whenever option #1 is used: "Father, by your power…," "Father, you have made…," "Father, by your plan…," keeping only the one paragraph which correspond to the readings you have chosen.

May she always follow the example of the holy women
whose praises are sung in the scriptures.

May her husband put his trust in her
and recognize that she is his equal
and the heir with him to the life of grace.
May he always honor her and love her
as Christ loves his bride, the Church.

Father, keep them always true to your commandments.
Keep them faithful in marriage
and let them be living examples of Christian life.

Give them the strength which comes from the gospel
so that they may be witnesses of Christ to others.
(Bless them with children
and help them to be good parents.
May they live to see their children's children.)
And, after a happy old age,
grant them fullness of life with the saints
in the kingdom of heaven.

We ask this through Christ our Lord.

2. Let us pray to the Lord for *N.* and *N.*
who come to God's altar at the beginning
   of their married life
so that they will always be united in love for each other
(as now they share in the body and blood of Christ).

Holy Father, you created mankind in your own image
and made man and woman to be joined
   as husband and wife
in union of body and heart
and so fulfill their mission in this world.

Father, to reveal the plan of your love,
you made the union of husband and wife
an image of the covenant between you
   and your people.

In the fulfillment of this sacrament,
the marriage of Christian man and woman
is a sign of the marriage between Christ
   and the Church.
Father, stretch out your hand, and bless *N.* and *N.*

Note:

In option #2 for the nuptial blessing, "as now they share in the body and blood of Christ" is omitted when the wedding is celebrated outside of Mass. Either the paragraph beginning with "Holy Father, you created mankind…" or the paragraph beginning with "Father, to reveal the plan of your love…" may be omitted, keeping only the paragraph which corresponds to the readings you have chosen.

Lord,
grant that as they begin to live this sacrament
they may share with each other the gifts of your love
and become one in heart and mind
as witnesses to your presence in their marriage.
Help them to create a home together
(and give them children to be formed by the gospel
and to have a place in your family).

Give your blessings to *N.*, your daughter,
so that she may be a good wife (and mother),
caring for the home,
faithful in love for her husband,
generous and kind.
Give your blessings to *N.*, your son,
so that he may be a faithful husband
(and a good father).

Father, grant that as they come together
    to your table on earth,
so they may one day have the joy of
sharing your feast in heaven.

We ask this through Christ our Lord.

3. My dear friends, let us ask God
for his continued blessings upon this
    bridegroom and his bride (or *N.* and *N.*).

Holy Father, creator of the universe,
maker of man and woman in your own likeness,
source of blessing for married life,
we humbly pray to you for this woman
who today is united with her husband in
    this sacrament of marriage.

May your fullest blessing come upon her
    and her husband
so that they may together rejoice in your
    gift of married love
(and enrich your Church with their children).

Lord,
may they both praise you when they are happy
and turn to you in their sorrows.
May they be glad that you help them in their work
and know that you are with them in their need.

WHO MAY RECEIVE COMMUNION?

To share in eating the Eucharistic Bread and drinking from the cup of the Eucharist is the preeminent sign of unity for Christians. It is the most intimate experience of union with God and with one another in the Church's tradition. This is the meaning of the word "Communion." Unfortunately, the current situation among Christians is one of disunity. There are Protestant, Orthodox and Catholic Churches, rather than one Christian Church. The guidelines for Communion in the Roman Catholic Church reflect this situation: since the various Churches are not united, it would be a false sign for Catholics to share the Eucharist with Christians who are not Catholic, a practice called "inter-Communion."

It is precisely because inter-Communion is not permitted that a wedding Mass is not encouraged when a Catholic marries someone who is not Catholic. The Eucharist would, in these weddings, be a sign of disunity at a time when the focus is on unity. A wedding outside of Mass is just as complete and is usually a more honest choice when a Catholic marries someone from another religious tradition.

In 1993, the Vatican issued a new ecumenical directory which allows local bishops to permit a spouse who is not Catholic to receive

continued

May they pray to you in the community
   of the Church,
and be your witnesses in the world.
May they reach old age in the company of
   their friends,
and come at last to the kingdom of heaven.

We ask this through Christ our Lord.

The response in each case is: **Amen.**

Sign of Peace

The sign of peace in the liturgy is more than a simple greeting. It is an opportunity for the members of the assembly to express their love for one another while wishing one another the peace of Christ. The priest faces the assembly and says: **Let us offer each other the sign of peace.** All exchange a handshake, kiss or other gesture of peace, saying: **The peace of Christ be with you.**

Breaking of the Bread

After the sign of peace, those who will serve as extraordinary ministers of holy Communion come into the sanctuary and stand near the altar. They may bring the additional vessels to the altar. The priest then divides the Eucharistic Bread among the vessels. During this time, the assembly sings (or says) the following:

**Lamb of God, you take away the sins
of the world: have mercy on us.
Lamb of God, you take away the sins
of the world: have mercy on us.
Lamb of God, you take away the sins
of the world: grant us peace.**

Communion

The priest then introduces the Communion rite with the following:

Priest: **This is the Lamb of God**
who takes away the sins of the world.
Happy are those who are called to his supper.

All: **Lord, I am not worthy to receive you,**
but only say the word and I shall be healed.

The priest consumes the body and blood of Christ. Then, he offers the Sacrament to each of you, saying, **The body of Christ** or **The blood of Christ,** to which you respond **Amen.** Once you have received, the priest and extraordinary ministers of holy Communion begin to distribute Communion to the rest of the assembly. During this time, the assembly sings a Communion song. (See Chapter Four for specific suggestions.)

Communion under the forms of both bread and wine, or Communion under both kinds, is preferred to Communion under the form of bread alone. This ancient practice, which was reintroduced for regular use in the United States in 1984, is a fuller response to the words of Christ at the Last Supper: "take and eat…take and drink." Many parishes have now adopted this practice for all Sunday Masses. The wedding liturgy offers an especially appropriate opportunity to celebrate the eucharistic banquet in its fullest form. Each person receiving Communion is free to choose whether to receive Communion from the cup or not. Don't deny people this option by distributing Communion under the form of bread only.

Prayer after Communion

After Communion, all sit for a period of silent prayer. A post-Communion song may also be sung (see Chapter Four). Then, all stand and the priest says one of the following:

1. **Lord,**
   in your love
   you have given us this eucharist
   to unite us with one another and with you.
   As you have made *N.* **and** *N.*
   one in this sacrament of marriage
   (and in the sharing of the one bread and the one cup),

Who May Receive Communion?
continued

Communion at his or her wedding. In this case, the spouse who is not Catholic acknowledges the teachings of the Catholic Church regarding the Eucharist; that is, that Christ is really present in the Eucharist. Discuss this option with the priest if you are interested in pursuing it.

The question of who may receive Communion also arises in weddings involving two Catholics but where a number of people from other religious traditions will be in the assembly. Two things should be kept in mind here: (1) since inter-Communion is not permitted, it is not appropriate to publicly invite those who are not Catholic to receive the Eucharist at a wedding Mass; (2) at the same time, it is inhospitable and not necessary to announce that those who are not Catholic may not receive the Eucharist at a wedding Mass. In other words, the current Church regulations should be respected, but there is no need to make announcements about the regulations within the liturgy or in the printed order of celebration. Ultimately the decision to receive the Eucharist always rests with the individual person.

If the regulations concerning inter-Communion are disturbing, they should be. They reflect a deeper scandal: the disunity of the Christian Church that Jesus sought to be one. It's all the more reason to pray for the unity of the Church in the prayer of the faithful and to pay special attention to making those who are not Catholic feel welcome at your wedding liturgy.

so now make them one in love for each other.

We ask this through Christ our Lord.

2. Lord,
   we who have shared the food of your table
   pray for our friends *N.* and *N.*,
   whom you have joined together in marriage.
   Keep them close to you always.
   May their love for each other
   proclaim to all the world
   their faith in you.

   We ask this through Christ our Lord.

3. Almighty God,
   may the sacrifice we have offered
   and the eucharist we have shared
   strengthen the love of *N.* and *N.*,
   and give us all your fatherly aid.

   We ask this through Christ our Lord.

The response in each case is: **Amen.**

THE CONCLUDING RITES

Final Blessing

The priest or deacon says, **The Lord be with you,** to which all respond, **And also with you.** (This response may be changed to **And with your spirit** as additional revisions are introduced into the Catholic liturgy.) Then, the priest or deacon says one of the following blessing prayers:

1. **God the eternal Father keep you in love
   with each other,
   so that the peace of Christ may stay with you
   and be always in your home.**

   All respond: **Amen.**

   **May (your children bless you,)
   your friends console you
   and all men live in peace with you.**

   All respond: **Amen.**

May you always bear witness to the love
    of God in this world
so that the afflicted and the needy
will find in you generous friends,
and welcome you into the joys of heaven.

All respond: **Amen.**

And may almighty God bless you all,
the Father, and the Son, † and the Holy Spirit.

All respond: **Amen.**

2. May God, the almighty Father,
   give you his joy
   and bless you (in your children).

   All respond: **Amen.**

   May the only Son of God have mercy on you
   and help you in good times and in bad.

   All respond: **Amen.**

   May the Holy Spirit of God
   always fill your hearts with his love.

   All respond: **Amen.**

   And may almighty God bless you all,
   the Father, and the Son, † and the Holy Spirit.

   All respond: **Amen.**

3. May the Lord Jesus, who was a guest at
       the wedding in Cana,
   bless you and your families and friends.

   All respond: **Amen.**

   May Jesus, who loved his church to the end,
   always fill your hearts with his love.

   All respond: **Amen.**

   May he grant that, as you believe in his resurrection,
   so you may wait for him in joy and hope.

   All respond: **Amen.**

   And may almighty God bless you all,
   the Father, and the Son, † and the Holy Spirit.

   All respond: **Amen.**

INVOLVING CHILDREN FROM A PREVIOUS MARRIAGE

Every marriage creates a new family from two existing families. The Church acknowledges and honors this reality by recommending that the parents of the bride and groom accompany the bride and groom in the entrance procession of the wedding liturgy.

Today it is not unusual for the bride and/or the groom to have children from a previous marriage. These children are part of the new family that is created by marriage. It is important to pay attention to their feelings about the upcoming marriage and to help them express their involvement in this new family. Lynn Brugnolotti, a parish music minister in North Carolina, has developed a simple yet profound way for children to take an active role in their parents' wedding:

Immediately before the final blessing, the priest or deacon invites the children forward with the following introduction:

A wedding is viewed as a union between two people. In reality, it is much more. As we give thanks to God for the love which brings *N.* and *N.* together, we recognize the merging of families this represents,

continued

4. **May almighty God, with his Word of blessing, unite your hearts in the never-ending bond of pure love.**

All respond: **Amen.**

May your children bring you happiness, and may your generous love for them be returned to you, many times over.

All respond: **Amen.**

**May the peace of Christ live always in your hearts and in your home.
May you have true friends to stand by you, both in joy and in sorrow.
May you be ready and willing to help and comfort all who come to you in need.
And may the blessings promised to the compassionate be yours in abundance.**

All respond: **Amen.**

**May you find happiness and satisfaction in your work.
May daily problems never cause you undue anxiety, nor the desire for earthly possessions dominate your lives.
But may your hearts' first desire be always the good things waiting for you in the life of heaven.**

All respond: **Amen.**

**May the Lord bless you with many happy years together, so that you may enjoy the rewards of a good life.
And after you have served him loyally in his kingdom on earth,
may he welcome you to his eternal kingdom in heaven.**

All respond: **Amen.**

And may almighty God bless you all, the Father, and the Son, † and the Holy Spirit.

All respond: **Amen.**

Solemn blessings, such as these, which are interspersed with **Amen** responses by the assembly, may be unfamiliar to many worshippers, including Roman Catholics. As a result, oftentimes few people make the **Amen** responses during the blessing. In light of this, two suggestions are offered: (a) have someone—the leader of song or the two of you—lead the **Amen** responses from a microphone; or (b) omit all but the final **Amen** response. The priest or deacon may also sing the final blessing. In this case, the leader of song would lead the assembly in singing the **Amen** responses.

Although not mentioned in the *Rite of Marriage,* a custom in some parishes for the final blessing is to ask the assembly to join the priest or deacon in blessing the couple. To do this, the two of you face the assembly, and the priest or deacon stands at the head of the assembly facing you. All extend their arms toward you as the priest or deacon recites the blessing prayer. (See Sample Program #2 on page 113 for an example of this.)

Dismissal

After the final blessing, the priest or deacon dismisses the assembly with one of the following:

1. **Go in the peace of Christ.**

2. **The Mass is ended, go in peace.**

3. **Go in peace to love and serve the Lord.**

The response in each case is: **Thanks be to God.**

Recessional

The recessional is a simple procession out of the church. The two of you go first, followed by the best man and maid/matron of honor and the ushers and bridesmaids. The priest or deacon may follow you, or he may remain in the sanctuary. An upbeat, festive piece of music is most effective to accompany this simple procession and to serve as a bridge to the continuation of the wedding celebration at the reception (see Chapter Four).

**Involving Children from a
Previous Marriage**
continued

with the additional love and responsibility. I now ask (children's names) to join us here for the final blessing.

The children come and stand next to their mother and/or father, and the presiding minister then prays final blessing #4. The children join in the recessional procession as part of this new family.

This simple gesture helps the children to feel much more a part of the wedding and the creation of this new family.

Note:

Option #2 for the dismissal is only used at weddings within Mass.

CHAPTER THREE

THE READINGS:
THE LECTIONARY
FOR MARRIAGE

Selecting the Scripture readings to be proclaimed at your wedding liturgy gives you an opportunity to share with one another some of the deepest values you hold. Take time with these readings to ponder the mystery of Christian marriage in light of God's revelation to us. The text of the reading appears first, followed by commentary to stimulate your thoughts. Some of the names that appear in certain readings are a real challenge to one's pronunciation skills, so a guide to pronunciation is provided for some of the more unfamiliar names.

It is customary to have three Scripture readings in the wedding liturgy: one from the Hebrew Scriptures (Old Testament), one from the writings of the apostles in the New Testament, and one from the Gospels. For pastoral reasons which might be discussed with the priest or deacon, it may be possible to omit one of the first two readings. Between the first and second readings, a Psalm is sung. If it is not possible to sing the Psalm, it may be recited. (The Psalms for weddings and information about appropriate musical settings are in Chapter Four.)

Some couples ask about the possibility of using readings from sources other than the Scriptures in the wedding liturgy. While such readings may reflect valuable insight into marriage, they are best used outside of the liturgy, for example at the rehearsal dinner or as part of a prayer or blessing before the meal at the reception. The readings in the wedding liturgy are limited to those that the Church holds to be the Word of God, that is, the Scriptures.

The Gospel is always proclaimed by either the priest or deacon who is the presiding minister at your wedding. This is the only Scripture reading that he should read. The other readings should be proclaimed by other people, either trained readers from the parish or friends or family members. Take special care that the people you choose as readers have a gift for reading in public or will work hard to proclaim the text well. Planning the roles friends and relatives will exercise in your wedding liturgy can be tricky business indeed. You don't want to hurt feelings, but neither do you want to embarrass someone who may not be gifted with an ability to read well in public.

Once you have chosen the readers, get the text of the readings to them in plenty of time to practice. Ideally, one person should proclaim the first reading, and someone else the second reading. If, however, you can identify only one good reader among the people who will be at your wedding, this person may proclaim both readings. At the rehearsal, be sure that the readers have a chance to read from the ambo that will be used at the wedding, with the amplification system turned on. (The ambo, which is sometimes called the lectern, is the stand from which Scripture readings are proclaimed during the liturgy.) Do not allow the readers to read from a simple sheet of paper or from this book during the liturgy. The Word of God should be in a dignified and substantial binding. The parish will have a bound copy of the Scripture readings for liturgy (called a lectionary) in which the priest, deacon or wedding coordinator can locate the readings you have chosen.

After the wedding is over, hold onto this book to use for discussion, sharing of insights, and praying together in the months and years ahead. Certain readings which do not appeal to you now might hold wonderful insight for you later as your experience of marriage deepens.

OPTIONS FOR THE READING FROM THE OLD TESTAMENT

OT-1: Genesis 1:26–28, 31a

1. *Male and female he created them.*

A reading from the Book of Genesis   1:26–28, 31a

Then God said: "Let us make man in our image, after our likeness. Let them have dominion over the fish of the sea, the birds of the air, and the cattle, and over all the wild animals and all the creatures that crawl on the ground."

God created man in his image;
in the image of God he created him;
male and female he created them.

God blessed them, saying: "Be fertile and multiply; fill the earth and subdue it. Have dominion over the fish of the sea, the birds of the air, and all the living things that move on the earth." God looked at everything he had made, and he found it very good.

The word of the Lord.

Commentary

There are two accounts of the creation of the world and of humankind in Genesis. In this first account, the creation of man and woman represents the climax of creation; they are created in the image and likeness of God, man and woman together constituting this image and likeness of God. The wonderful dignity of man and woman is taught in this story as well as their complementarity, the essence of the gift of sexuality which God pronounced very good.

OT-2: Genesis 2:18–24

2. *The two of them become one body.*

A reading from the Book of Genesis   2:18–24

The LORD God said: "It is not good for the man to be alone. I will make a suitable partner for him." So the LORD God formed out of the ground various wild animals and various birds of the air, and he brought them to the man to see what he would call them; whatever the man called each of them would be its name. The man gave names to all the cattle, all the birds of the air, and all wild animals; but none proved to be the suitable partner for the man. So the LORD God cast a deep sleep on the man, and while he was asleep, he took out one of his ribs and closed up its place with flesh. The LORD God then built up into a woman the rib that he had taken from the man. When he brought her to the man, the man said:

"This one, at last, is bone of my bones
    and flesh of my flesh;
This one shall be called 'woman,'
    for out of 'her man' this one has been taken."

That is why a man leaves his father and mother and clings to his wife, and the two of them become one body.

The word of the Lord.

Commentary

This is the second and, according to today's standards, less popular account of creation. In the past, this description of the creation of the first woman from the rib of man was sometimes used to point up the subordination of woman to man as his helpmate. But contemporary scholars point out that the Hebrew word for help does not indicate subordination. It is used, for example, of God as the helper of Israel. The version of the Bible which is used in Catholic liturgy translates helpmate properly as partner. This story might be used if the wedding homily were to teach of the sanctity of physical creation, including human sexuality. Man and woman in marriage are to be one flesh; so it has been ordained by God.

OT-3: Genesis 24:48–51, 58–67

3. *In his love for Rebekah, Isaac found solace after the death of his mother.*

A reading from the Book of Genesis   24:48–51, 58–67

The servant of Abraham said to Laban: "I bowed down in worship to the LORD, blessing the LORD, the God of my master Abraham, who had led me on the right road to obtain the daughter of my master's kinsman for his son. If, therefore, you have in mind to show true loyalty to my master, let me know; but if not, let me know that, too. I can then proceed accordingly."

Laban and his household said in reply: "This thing comes from the LORD; we can say nothing to you either for or against it. Here is Rebekah, ready for you; take her with you, that she may become the wife of your master's son, as the LORD has said."

So they called Rebekah and asked her, "Do you wish to go with this man?" She answered, "I do." At this they allowed their sister Rebekah and her nurse to take leave, along with Abraham's servant and his men. Invoking a blessing on Rebekah, they said:

"Sister, may you grow
    into thousands of myriads;
And may your descendants gain possession
    of the gates of their enemies!"

Then Rebekah and her maids started out; they mounted their camels and followed the man. So the servant took Rebekah and went on his way.

56

Meanwhile Isaac had gone from Beer-lahai-roi and was living in the region of the Negeb. One day toward evening he went out… in the field, and as he looked around, he noticed that camels were approaching. Rebekah, too, was looking about, and when she saw him, she alighted from her camel and asked the servant, "Who is the man out there, walking through the fields toward us?" "That is my master," replied the servant. Then she covered herself with her veil.

The servant recounted to Isaac all the things he had done. Then Isaac took Rebekah into his tent; he married her, and thus she became his wife. In his love for her Isaac found solace after the death of his mother Sarah.

The word of the Lord.

Pronunciation notes:

Laban = LAY – b'n

Beerlahairoi – BEE – er – luh – HAY – roy

Negeb = NEH – geb

Isaac = EYE – zik

Commentary

Many of the people at your wedding will not be familiar with this story. In order for the reading to make sense, the homilist will need to explain the verses in chapter 24 that precede it. If that is done, this reading will be revealed as a beautiful reading which emphasizes how Yahweh proved his fidelity by providing an appropriate wife for Abraham's son, Isaac. The first of the three nuptial blessings from the *Rite of Marriage* (see page 43) mentions the holy women whose praises were sung in the Scriptures. Rebekah was one of those holy women. This reading might be used to stress God's fidelity to you in marriage as well as the importance of the companionship and consolation husband and wife can offer each other in difficult times. So, it should be, as Rebekah consoled Isaac after the loss of his mother.

OT-4: Tobit 7:6–14

4. *May the Lord of heaven prosper you both.*
   May he grant you mercy and peace.

A reading from the Book of Tobit   7:6–14

Raphael and Tobiah entered the house of Raguel and greeted him. Raguel sprang up and kissed Tobiah, shedding tears of joy. But when he heard that Tobit had lost his eyesight, he was grieved and wept aloud. He said to Tobiah: "My child, God bless you! You are the son of a noble and good father. But what a terrible misfortune that such a righteous and charitable man should be afflicted with blindness!" He continued to weep in the arms of his kinsman Tobiah. His wife Edna also wept for Tobit; and even their daughter Sarah began to weep.

Afterward, Raguel slaughtered a ram from the flock and gave them a cordial reception. When they had bathed and reclined to eat, Tobiah said to Raphael, "Brother Azariah, ask Raguel to let me marry my kinswoman Sarah." Raguel overheard the words; so he said to the boy: "Eat and drink and be merry tonight, for no man is more entitled to marry my daughter Sarah than you, brother. Besides, not even I have the right to give her to anyone but you, because you are my closest relative. But I will explain the situation to you very frankly. I have given her in marriage to seven men, all of whom were kinsmen of ours, and all died on the very night they approached her. But now, son, eat and drink. I am sure the Lord will look after you both." Tobiah answered, "I will eat or drink nothing until you set aside what belongs to me."

Raguel said to him: "I will do it. She is yours according to the decree of the Book of Moses. Your marriage to her has been decided in heaven! Take your kinswoman from now on you are her love, and she is your beloved. She is yours today and ever after. And tonight, son, may the Lord of heaven prosper you both. May he grant you mercy and peace." Then Raguel called his daughter Sarah, and she came to him. He took her by the hand and gave her to Tobiah with the words: "Take her according to the law. According to the decree written in the Book of Moses she is your wife. Take her and bring her back safely to your father. And may the God of heaven grant both of you peace and prosperity." He then called her mother and told her to bring a scroll, so that he might draw up a marriage contract stating that he gave Sarah to Tobiah as his wife according to the decree of the Mosaic law. Her mother brought the scroll, and he drew up the contract, to which they affixed their seals.

Afterward they began to eat and drink.

The word of the Lord.

Pronunciation notes:

Tobit = TOE – bit

Tobiah = Toe – BUY – ah

Raphael = RAY – fay – el

Azariah = Az – uh – RYE – uh

Raguel = Rah – G'YOU – el

Mosaic = Moe - ZAY – ik

Commentary

This and the following reading from Tobit are parts of the same story. But as in the previous reading from Genesis, one needs to know something of the story of the Book of Tobit to grasp the full significance of these selections from the account. Tobit, a devout and charitable man, lived in exile at Ninevah. His kinsman Raguel lived at Ecbatana. Each had a serious problem. Tobit was blind and Raguel's daughter Sarah had seven bridegrooms in succession killed on the wedding night by the demon Asmodeus. God heard the prayer of Tobit and Sarah; he sent Tobit's son Tobiah to Raguel, married him to Sarah (and he was *not* killed on the wedding night) and gave him a cure for his father's blindness. The story is a lesson in hope, perseverance and trust in God even in seemingly hopeless circumstances. The story has a certain human warmth and gentle humor. Tobit's talk of following the law of Moses refers to the patriarchal custom of keeping marriage within the clan. Making God and trust in God the foundation of your marriage is a formula for success.

OT-5: Tobit 8:4b–8

5. *Allow us to live together to a happy old age.*

A reading from the Book of Tobit   8:4b–8

On their wedding night Tobiah arose from bed and said to his wife, "Sister, get up. Let us pray and beg our Lord to have mercy on us and to grant us deliverance." Sarah got up, and they started to pray and beg that deliverance might be theirs. They began with these words:

"Blessed are you, O God of our fathers;
**   praised be your name forever and ever.**
Let the heavens and all your creation
**   praise you forever.**
You made Adam and you gave him his wife Eve
**   to be his help and support;**
**   and from these two the human race descended.**
You said, 'It is not good for the man to be alone;
**   let us make him a partner like himself.'**
Now, Lord, you know that I take this wife of mine
**   not because of lust,**
**   but for a noble purpose.**
Call down your mercy on me and on her,
**   and allow us to live together to a happy old age."**

They said together, "Amen, amen."

The word of the Lord.

Commentary

If one knows of Sarah's experience on her seven previous wedding nights, one can understand the urgency of both Sarah's and Tobiah's prayer. It is a lovely scene. Tobiah shows great respect for Sarah in his prayer. God created man and woman to be companions, partners. So he does not take her for any lustful motive, but in singleness of heart. To love each other with singleness of heart is a grace to be sought for in every marriage. And it is one God fully intends to grant, because fidelity and love in marriage are ordained to point to the faithful love of God for us. Marriage is to be a mystery pointing to the mysterious union of Christ with his Church (see NT-6).

OT-6: Proverbs 31:10–13, 19–20, 30–31

6. *The woman who fears the Lord is to be praised.*

A reading from the Book of Proverbs   31:10–13, 19–20, 30–31

When one finds a worthy wife,
  her value is far beyond pearls.
Her husband, entrusting his heart to her,
  has an unfailing prize.
She brings him good, and not evil,
  all the days of her life.
She obtains wool and flax
  and makes cloth with skillful hands.
She puts her hands to the distaff,
  and her fingers ply the spindle.
She reaches out her hands to the poor,
  and extends her arms to the needy.
Charm is deceptive and beauty fleeting;
  the woman who fears the LORD is to be praised.
Give her a reward of her labors,
  and let her works praise her at the city gates.

The word of the Lord.

Commentary

Proverbs is an anthology of didactic poetry designed to inform and train the young about making good choices, and partly to provide advanced training in wisdom. This passage speaks of finding a "woman of worth," extolling her value in practical, domestic terms. She is a priceless gift, not only to her husband, but to the needy to whom "she extends her arms."

There is another feminine entity, Wisdom, which is extolled in the first nine chapters of the same Book of Proverbs. If you read the later passage through the lens of the earlier, the "woman of worth" is also the "woman of wisdom." This, of course, in addition to enhancing her mystery and attractiveness, enhances many fold her value to her husband.

"Happy the man who finds wisdom,
  the man who gains understanding!
For her profit is better than profit in silver,
  and better than gold is her revenue;
She is more precious than corals,
  and none of your choice possessions can compare with her."
(Proverbs 3:13–15)

60

If husband and wife were alert not so much to the charm or beauty of the other but to the wisdom the other gained through the years, wouldn't their interest in one another keep advancing year after year?

OT-7: Song of Songs 2:8–10, 14, 16a; 8:6–7a

7. *Stern as death is love.*

A reading from the Song of Songs   2:8–10, 14, 16a; 8:6–7a

> **Hark! my lover—here he comes**
> **springing across the mountains,**
> **leaping across the hills.**
> **My lover is like a gazelle**
> **or a young stag.**
> **Here he stands behind our wall,**
> **gazing through the windows,**
> **peering through the lattices.**
> **My lover speaks; he says to me,**
> **"Arise, my beloved, my dove, my beautiful one, and come!**
>
> **"O my dove in the clefts of the rock,**
> **in the secret recesses of the cliff,**
> **Let me see you,**
> **let me hear your voice,**
> **For your voice is sweet,**
> **and you are lovely."**
>
> **My lover belongs to me and I to him.**
> **He says to me:**
>
> **"Set me as a seal on your heart,**
> **as a seal on your arm;**
> **For stern as death is love,**
> **relentless as the nether-world is devotion;**
> **its flames are a blazing fire.**
> **Deep waters cannot quench love,**
> **nor floods sweep it away."**

The word of the Lord.

Commentary

Some commentators, both Jewish and Christian, interpret the Song of Songs, which means 'the greatest of all songs," allegorically. That is, they see the relationship of lover and beloved in the poems as pointing to various moments in the love relationship between God and Israel or between Christ and the Church. Other scholars see the book as a collection of hymns to true love sanctified by union. The inclusion of the Song of Songs in the canon of holy Scripture leads us to interpret the work as an analogy of the love of God for us; this interpretation also affirms the goodness and sanctity of sexual love. The passionate love of God for us is a mystery as is the passionate love of man and woman. It is as strong as death. The love of God for us in Christ conquered death forever and God's Spirit of love given to us is the guarantee of our living and loving forever.

OT-8: Sirach 26:1–4, 13–16

8. *Like the sun rising in the LORD's heavens,*
   the beauty of a virtuous wife is the radiance of her home.

A reading from the Book of Sirach   26:1–4, 13–16

Blessed the husband of a good wife,
**   twice-lengthened are his days;**
A worthy wife brings joy to her husband,
**   peaceful and full is his life.**
A good wife is a generous gift
**   bestowed upon him who fears the LORD;**
Be he rich or poor, his heart is content,
**   and a smile is ever on his face.**

A gracious wife delights her husband,
**   her thoughtfulness puts flesh on his bones;**
A gift from the LORD is her governed speech,
**   and her firm virtue is of surpassing worth.**
Choicest of blessings is a modest wife,
**   priceless her chaste soul.**
A holy and decent woman adds grace upon grace;
**   indeed, no price is worthy of her temperate soul.**
Like the sun rising in the LORD's heavens,
**   the beauty of a virtuous wife is the radiance of her home.**

The word of the Lord.

Pronunciation note:
    Sirach = SEER – ak

Commentary

Much of the Book of Sirach consists of advice from a father to his son and includes advice on sex and marriage. No doubt, many couples today will not choose this reading given the viewpoint taken in it. The selection is a description of a good wife from the husband's point of view which seems to place too great an emphasis on her function to provide him happiness. Roles and relationships change in society. But even in the second century before Christ, which is reflected in this reading, the centrality of one's marriage partner in one's life is clearly spelled out. There is a lesson here for us today when often two careers in one household, or the temptation to materialism which financial security and affluence brings, puts serious stresses on marriage relationships and tempts one to think that one's marriage partner is just one among many important things in one's life. That is not the message in Sirach.

OT-9: Jeremiah 31:31–32a, 33–34a

9. *I will make a new covenant with the house of Israel and the house of Judah.*

A reading from the Book of the Prophet Jeremiah   31:31–32a, 33–34a

The days are coming, says the LORD, when I will make a new covenant with the house of Israel and the house of Judah. It will not be like the covenant I made with their fathers: the day I took them by the hand to lead them forth from the land of Egypt. But this is the covenant which I will make with the house of Israel after those days, says the LORD. I will place my law within them, and write it upon their hearts; I will be their God, and they shall be my people. No longer will they have need to teach their friends and relatives how to know the LORD. All, from least to greatest, shall know me, says the LORD.

The word of the Lord.

Pronunciation note:

Jeremiah = Jer – eh – MY – uh

Commentary

For the nomadic peoples of the desert, a covenant was a bond as strong as blood. The welfare of a covenant partner meant as much to you as your own welfare; whenever in need, what is mine is yours, what is yours is mine. The covenant in this reading from Jeremiah is that promised to Israel as the people of God and fulfilled, according to Christian faith, in Christ. If you choose this for the first reading and Ephesians (see NT-6) for the second, you would highlight the relationship between God's covenant with his people and the marriage covenant. It is the faith of the Church that marriage is the privileged place where the covenant of God's love may be most effectively embodied among God's people. Marriage covenant love ought to be a pledge and an anticipation of the love shown in the kingdom of heaven. Marriage is, in a true sense, a herald announcing that kingdom.

OPTIONS FOR THE READING FROM THE NEW TESTAMENT

NT-1: Romans 8:31b–35, 37–39

1. *What will separate us from the love of Christ?*

A reading from the Letter of Saint Paul to the Romans   8:31b–35, 37–39

Brothers and sisters: If God is for us, who can be against us? He did not spare his own Son but handed him over for us all, will he not also give us everything else along with him? Who will bring a charge against God's chosen ones? It is God who acquits us. Who will condemn? It is Christ Jesus who died, rather, was raised, who also is at the right hand of God, who indeed intercedes for us. What will separate us from the love of Christ? Will anguish, or distress, or persecution, or famine, or nakedness, or peril, or the sword?

No, in all these things, we conquer overwhelmingly through him who loved us. For I am convinced that neither death, nor life, nor angels, nor principalities, nor present things, nor future things, nor powers, nor height, nor depth, nor any other creature will be able to separate us from the love of God in Christ Jesus our Lord.

The word of the Lord.

Commentary

For Saint Paul, the power of the love of God was demonstrated by the obedient death of Jesus on the cross. The death and resurrection of Jesus was the definitive victory over all of life's troubles, including death, so that nothing in the future can interfere with God's love for us; nothing can take us out of God's reach. God's powerful and unconditional love is the ideal of love married persons should strive for: first between themselves, then for all their brothers and sisters. While this reading fits well into any series of readings in the marriage Lectionary, it might be very fitting after the reading from the Song of Songs (OT-7). It is difficult for humans to imagine the depth and breadth of God's unconditional love for them; we are so conscious of our own limits, our pride and self-centeredness. But we must resist the temptation to model God's love on our own and rather strive to model our love on God's, relying on the Spirit who is love to empower us.

NT-2: Romans 12:1–2, 9–18

2. LONG FORM

Offer your bodies as a living sacrifice, holy and pleasing to God.

A reading from the Letter of Saint Paul to the Romans   12:1–2, 9–18

I urge you, brothers and sisters, by the mercies of God, to offer your bodies as a living sacrifice, holy and pleasing to God, your spiritual worship. Do not conform yourselves to this age but be transformed by the renewal of your mind, that you may discern what is the will of God, what is good and pleasing and perfect.

Let love be sincere; hate what is evil, hold on to what is good; love one another with mutual affection; anticipate one another in showing honor. Do not grow slack in zeal, be fervent in spirit, serve the Lord. Rejoice in hope, endure in affliction, persevere in prayer. Contribute to the needs of the holy ones, exercise hospitality. Bless those who persecute you, bless and do not curse them. Rejoice with those who rejoice, weep with those who weep. Have the same regard for one another; do not be haughty but associate with the lowly; do not be wise in your own estimation. Do not repay anyone evil for evil; be concerned for what is noble in the sight of all. If possible, on your part, live at peace with all.

The word of the Lord.

OR

Offer your bodies as a living sacrifice, holy and pleasing to God.

A reading from the Letter of Saint Paul to the Romans   12:1–2, 9–13

I urge you, brothers and sisters, by the mercies of God, to offer your bodies as a living sacrifice, holy and pleasing to God, your spiritual worship. Do not conform yourselves to this age but be transformed by the renewal of your mind, that you may discern what is the will of God, what is good and pleasing and perfect.

Let love be sincere; hate what is evil, hold on to what is good; love one another with mutual affection; anticipate one another in showing honor. Do not grow slack in zeal, be fervent in spirit, serve the Lord. Rejoice in hope, endure in affliction, persevere in prayer. Contribute to the needs of the holy ones, exercise hospitality.

The word of the Lord.

Commentary

Paul urges the Christians at Rome to put their beliefs into practice so that their Christian behavior might become a sacrifice to God. He follows this with a warning not to model their lives on the behavior patterns of the world. Married couples would do well to frame this passage on Christian love and pray over it daily. Paul includes hospitality among the qualities Christians should manifest; this is a special virtue of married couples who should not be turned in on themselves, but make their home a place of welcome for others. In our society which encourages expectations of affluent living, our dreams of the future should encompass the welfare of all people, especially the poor, not just our own families.

NT-3: Romans 15:1b-3a, 5–7, 13

3. *Welcome one another as Christ welcomed you.*

A reading from the Letter of Saint Paul to the Romans   15:1b–3a, 5–7, 13

Brothers and sisters: We ought to put up with the failings of the weak and not to please ourselves; let each of us please our neighbor for the good, for building up. For Christ did not please himself. May the God of endurance and encouragement grant you to think in harmony with one another, in keeping with Christ Jesus, that with one accord you may with one voice glorify the God and Father of our Lord Jesus Christ.

Welcome one another, then, as Christ welcomed you, for the glory of God. May the God of hope fill you with all joy and peace in believing, so that you may abound in hope by the power of the Holy Spirit.

The word of the Lord.

Commentary

This passage offers some tough but vital advice to those entering marriage. Here's why: married people, over time, get to appreciate one another's strengths. Inevitably, however, they also discover one another's weaknesses with a clarity they did not have on the day of their wedding. When this happens in their relationship, when they are surprised, disappointed and, perhaps, worried, they should read and be strengthened by this passage from Saint Paul, starting with his prayer: "May the God of hope fill you with all joy and peace...." Have hope, he says, that the Holy Spirit will empower you to love one another well.

This means that, when necessary, you can "put up with the failings of the weak." The primary literal meaning of the Greek word translated here as "put up with" is actually much stronger. It means "support" or "carry." It seems that Paul is asking for more than toleration; rather, he is asking for serious, sustained assistance for the weak. And his next phrases show that he understands what that will sometimes ask of the partner: we ought "not to please ourselves; let each of us please our neighbor for the good, for building up."

This can be a tall order. But, lucky for us, Christian marriage is not limited to reliance on one's own resources to make it successful. Christ, "who did not please himself," has won for us and shared with us the power of the Holy Spirit. Our God is a god "of endurance and encouragement" who shares those dispositions with us so that we may endure difficulties for the sake of one another and be able to encourage one another when one's weaknesses challenge one's hope.

The meaning of God's gift to us in Jesus Christ is that if we die to ourselves out of love, we can discover a deeper, fuller life both here and hereafter. "Welcome one another, then, as Christ welcomed you, for the glory of God."

NT-4: 1 Corinthians 6:13c–15a, 17–20

4. *Your body is a temple of the Spirit.*

A reading from the first Letter of Saint Paul to the Corinthians   6:13c–15a, 17–20

Brothers and sisters: The body is not for immorality, but for the Lord, and the Lord is for the body; God raised the Lord and will also raise us by his power.

Do you not know that your bodies are members of Christ? Whoever is joined to the Lord becomes one spirit with him. Avoid immorality. Every other sin a person commits is outside the body, but the immoral person sins against his own body. Do you not know that your body is a temple of the Holy Spirit within you, whom you have from God, and that you are not your own? For you have been purchased at a price. Therefore glorify God in your body.

The word of the Lord.

Pronunciation note:

Corinthians = Cor – IN – thee – enz

Commentary

Do not be put off by Paul's chastening tone; the passage contains a very important Christian affirmation: the flesh and all material creation are holy and belong to the Lord. Paul uses two images to stress the sanctity of the human body: he reminds the Christians that their bodies are members of Christ's body and that they are temples of the Holy Spirit. We are not our own; we have been bought and paid for by the life and death of Jesus. There is evidence that this reading was already in use in some Christian marriage services in the sixth century.

NT-5: 1 Corinthians 12:31—13:8a

5. *If I do not have love, I gain nothing.*

A reading from the first Letter of Saint Paul to the Corinthians   12:31—13:8a

Brothers and sisters: Strive eagerly for the greatest spiritual gifts.
But I shall show you a still more excellent way.
If I speak in human and angelic tongues but do not have love, I am a resounding gong or a clashing cymbal. And if I have the gift of prophecy and comprehend all mysteries and all knowledge; if I have all faith so as to move mountains, but do not have love, I am nothing. If I give away everything I own, and if I hand my body over so that I may boast but do not have love, I gain nothing.

Love is patient, love is kind. It is not jealous, is not pompous, it is not inflated, it is not rude, it does not seek its own interests, it is not quick-tempered, it does not brood over injury, it does not rejoice over wrongdoing but rejoices with the truth. It bears all things, believes all things, hopes all things, endures all things. Love never fails.

The word of the Lord.

Commentary

Paul teaches us that, while talent and knowledge are wonderful gifts, love is the one thing required of us in this life. But love is demanding; it encompasses patience, humility, selflessness, courtesy and respect. Love puts good interpretations on what others say and do; it does not resent others' success but rejoices in it and in the truth. Love is ready to forgive, to trust and to endure. Little more need to be said about the heart of a marriage relationship. But the source of such a love, which is promised to every couple in the sacrament of marriage, can only be God.

NT-6: Ephesians 5:2a, 21–33

6. LONG FORM

This is a great mystery, but I speak in reference to Christ and the Church.

A reading from the Letter of Saint Paul to the Ephesians   5:2a, 21–33

Brothers and sisters: Live in love, as Christ loved us and handed himself over for us.
Be subordinate to one another out of reverence for Christ. Wives should be subordinate to their husbands as to the Lord. For the husband is head of his wife just as Christ is head of the Church, he himself the savior of the body. As the Church is subordinate to Christ, so wives should be subordinate to their husbands in everything. Husbands, love your wives, even as Christ loved the Church and handed himself over for her to sanctify her, cleansing her by the bath of water with the word, that he might present to himself the Church in splendor, without spot or wrinkle or any such thing, that she might be holy and without blemish. So also husbands should love their wives as their own bodies. He who loves his wife loves himself. For no one hates his own flesh but rather nourishes and cherishes it, even as Christ does the Church, because we are members of his Body.

> **For this reason a man shall leave his father and his mother**
> **and be joined to his wife,**
> **and the two shall become one flesh.**

This is a great mystery, but I speak in reference to Christ and the Church. In any case, each one of you should love his wife as himself, and the wife should respect her husband.

The word of the Lord.

OR

This is a great mystery, but I speak in reference to Christ and the Church.

A reading from the Letter of Saint Paul to the Ephesians   5:2a, 25–32

Brothers and sisters: Live in love, as Christ loved us and handed himself over for us.

Husbands, love your wives, even as Christ loved the Church and handed himself over for her to sanctify her, cleansing her by the bath of water with the word, that he might present to himself the Church in splendor, without spot or wrinkle or any such thing, that she might be holy and without blemish. So also husbands should love their wives as their own bodies. He who loves his wife loves himself. For no one hates his own flesh but rather nourishes and cherishes it, even as Christ does the Church, because we are members of his Body.

> **For this reason a man shall leave his father and his mother**
> **and be joined to his wife,**
> **and the two shall become one flesh.**

This is a great mystery, but I speak in reference to Christ and the Church.

The word of the Lord.

Pronunciation note:
Ephesians = Eh – FEE – shenz

Commentary

This reading is part of what scholars call a household code. Taken by early Christianity from Hellenistic Judaism, these codes set forth the duties of husband, wives, parents, children, masters and slaves. In some cases the codes were borrowed almost without change, but this passage in Ephesians added a special elaboration on the meaning of marriage by comparing it to the relation between Christ and his Church. The reading reflects the subordinationist pattern of societal relationships in force at the time. Notice, however, that this is *not* the distinctly Christian element in the household code presented here. The Christian community, including our own, is never exempt from cultural conditioning. The inspiring heart of this passage, however, portrays the love of husband and wife as so special that it can be compared analogously to the great love of Christ for the Church.

NT-7: Philippians 4:4–9

7. *The God of peace will be with you.*

A reading from the Letter of Saint Paul to the Philippians   4:4–9

Brothers and sisters: Rejoice in the Lord always. I shall say it again: rejoice! Your kindness should be known to all. The Lord is near. Have no anxiety at all, but in everything, by prayer

and petition, with thanksgiving, make your requests known to God. Then the peace of God that surpasses all understanding will guard your hearts and minds in Christ Jesus.

Finally, brothers and sisters, whatever is true, whatever is honorable, whatever is just, whatever is pure, whatever is lovely, whatever is gracious, if there is any excellence and if there is anything worthy of praise, think about these things. Keep on doing what you have learned and received and heard and seen in me. Then the God of peace will be with you.

The word of the Lord.

Pronunciation note:

Philippians = Fih – LIP – ee – enz

Commentary

"For better, for worse, for richer, for poorer, in sickness and in health, don't worry!" This is what Saint Paul could be saying to you if you choose the Philippians passage for your wedding liturgy. He describes in a few lines the Christian formula for peace of heart in all circumstances. "Have no anxiety at all," he says.

Looking back on your experience of life so far and looking ahead to the challenges, known and unknown, in your life together, an anxiety-free life may seem like a fool's dream. Yet, that is what is promised us in this inspired reading.

The formula for peace sounds simple: pray. Pray, first of all, for stronger faith and trust that "the Lord is near." Pray for yourselves and for others. Don't hesitate to ask for what you need but (and this is the key to the formula) do it in a context of gratitude, of thanksgiving.

It can be correctly said that gratitude is the foundational Christian attitude. People who habitually count their blessings and give thanks to God are fundamentally peaceful people. Try it. Try living just one day conscious that all you are and have is pure gift. You will then understand why the central prayer of the Church is Eucharist—thanksgiving, reverent acknowledgement of God's dominion and extraordinary love.

The peace of God that surpasses all understanding does not mean simply the absence of conflict. It is deeper than that, a gift from God that is beyond our mind's calculations, yet is promised to those who are grateful and who pray.

NT-8: Colossians 3:12–17

8. *And over all these put on love,*
   that is, the bond of perfection.

A reading from the Letter of Saint Paul to the Colossians   3:12–17

Brothers and sisters: Put on, as God's chosen ones, holy and beloved, heartfelt compassion, kindness, humility, gentleness, and patience, bearing with one another and forgiving one another, if one has a grievance against another; as the Lord has forgiven you, so must you also do. And over all these put on love, that is, the bond of perfection. And let the peace of Christ control your hearts, the peace into which you were also called in one Body. And be thankful. Let the word of Christ dwell in you richly, as in all wisdom you teach and admonish one another, singing psalms, hymns, and spiritual songs with gratitude in your hearts to God. And whatever you do, in word or in deed, do everything in the name of the Lord Jesus, giving thanks to God the Father through him.

The word of the Lord.

Pronunciation note:

Colossians = Kuh – LOSH – enz

Commentary

This is another household code but some distinctive Christian elements in human relationships are highlighted in it. In the wedding liturgy, special emphasis might be placed on the special need of forgiveness in love relationships. It is God's love and forgiveness of us that is the reason for and the model of our forgiveness of one another. The author urges us to let the word of Christ dwell in us and to speak with each other with the wisdom granted us by the Spirit. Communication on a regular, sustained basis is absolutely essential to a healthy marriage.

NT-9: Hebrews 13:1–4a, 5–6b

9. *Let marriage be held in honor by all.*

A reading from the Letter to the Hebrews   13:1–4a, 5–6b

Brothers and sisters: Let mutual love continue. Do not neglect hospitality, for through it some have unknowingly entertained angels. Be mindful of prisoners as if sharing their imprisonment, and of the ill-treated as of yourselves, for you also are in the body. Let marriage be honored among all and the marriage bed be kept undefiled. Let your life be free from love of money but be content with what you have, for he has said, *I will never forsake you or abandon you.* Thus we may say with confidence:

The Lord is my helper,
and I will not be afraid.

The word of the Lord.

Commentary

These ethical admonitions at the conclusion of the letter to the Hebrews apply to all people, but for those entering marriage they are singularly appropriate: maintaining mutual love for one another, offering hospitality in your new home—your domestic church, not being so preoccupied with one another that you forget the marginalized and are unable to identify with them, fidelity to one another in sexual matters, being content with what you have, not making money more important than it deserves to be.

What supports this kind of Christian married life are the gifts of faith and trust in God's promises, such as: "I will never forsake you or abandon you." Clearly marriage, which should be honored by all, demands regular listening to the Word of God and celebration of the sacred mysteries entrusted to us so that one will be constantly reminded of how much God loves us and how faithful God has always been to the promises made to God's people. If a couple is grounded in gratitude to God, it is much easier for them in their married life to be light for one another and a sign of God's kingdom to the world.

NT-10: 1 Peter 3:1–9

10. *Be of one mind, sympathetic, loving toward one another.*

A reading from the first Letter of Saint Peter   3:1–9

Beloved: You wives should be subordinate to your husbands so that, even if some disobey the word, they may be won over without a word by their wives' conduct when they observe your reverent and chaste behavior. Your adornment should not be an external one: braiding the hair, wearing gold jewelry, or dressing in fine clothes, but rather the hidden character of the heart, expressed in the imperishable beauty of a gentle and calm disposition, which is precious in the sight of God. For this is also how the holy women who hoped in God once used to adorn themselves and were subordinate to their husbands; thus Sarah obeyed Abraham, calling him "lord." You are her children when you do what is good and fear no intimidation.

Likewise, you husbands should live with your wives in understanding, showing honor to the weaker female sex, since we are joint heirs of the gift of life, so that your prayers may not be hindered.

Finally, all of you, be of one mind, sympathetic, loving toward one another, compassionate, humble. Do not return evil for evil, or insult for insult; but, on the contrary, a blessing, because to this you were called, that you might inherit a blessing.

The word of the Lord.

Commentary

The first part of this household code is directed to Christian women whose spouses are pagan. It suggests that by their conduct they might win over their husbands to the faith. There follows a diatribe against the use of cosmetics! If one can make allowances for the cultural setting of this reading which calls woman "the weaker sex" and extols Sarah who called her husband her master, the reading does commend some important Christian virtues that every marriage relationship should take to heart, in particular, not returning wrong for wrong or anger for anger, but returning a blessing when one has been harmed. The successful marriage is one which seeks the truly good things in life: a forgiving atmosphere, peace in the home, fidelity and hospitality.

NT-11: 1 John 3:18–24

11. *Love in deed and in truth*

A reading from the first Letter of Saint John   3:18–24

Children, let us love not in word or speech but in deed and truth.
Now this is how we shall know that we belong to the truth and reassure our hearts before him in whatever our hearts condemn, for God is greater than our hearts and knows everything. Beloved, if our hearts do not condemn us, we have confidence in God and receive from him whatever we ask, because we keep his commandments and do what pleases him. And his commandment is this: we should believe in the name of his Son, Jesus Christ, and love one another just as he commanded us. Those who keep his commandments remain in him, and he in them, and the way we know that he remains in us is from the Spirit that he gave us.

The word of the Lord.

Commentary

If we do what God commands, we will abide in God. Sometimes it is not an easy thing to know what God's desires are for us or for others. This reading addresses this situation and reminds us that even if we are uncertain as to how we stand before God, we should trust that God understands us better than we know ourselves. If we have faith in Jesus and try to love one another as God loves us, we should be confident that God will care for us. Couples will have to make many decisions, the rightness or wrongness of which may not always be clear. A well informed conscience, marked by honesty, by careful inquiry and by prayer, will guarantee peace of mind. But our love must not reside in words alone; it must issue in deeds.

NT-12: 1 John 4:7–12

12. *God is love.*

A reading from the first Letter of Saint John   4:7–12

Beloved, let us love one another, because love is of God; everyone who loves is begotten by God and knows God. Whoever is without love does not know God, for God is love. In this way the love of God was revealed to us: God sent his only-begotten Son into the world so that we might have life through him. In this is love: not that we have loved God, but that he loved

us and sent his Son as expiation for our sins. Beloved, if God so loved us, we also must love one another. No one has ever seen God. Yet, if we love one another, God remains in us, and his love is brought to perfection in us.

The word of the Lord.

Commentary

The author can testify that the Christian community believes that God is love because they have seen and felt the Father's love in Jesus, his Son. Only the person who loves, the reading goes on to say, can truly know God because God is love. The invitation to love which marriage is, is an invitation to enter more deeply as time goes by into the mystery of your marriage partner and into the mystery that is God. It is the outpouring of God's love for us that brought us into being and enables us to live and love. Since we are made in God's image and likeness, we are called to imitate the love of God. Since God loved us first, we are called to love others first. We love others not because they love us, but because they are in themselves beautiful creations of our Father and worthy of our love as they are the objects of his.

NT-13: Revelation 19:1, 5–9a

13.   *Blessed are those who have been called to the wedding feast of the Lamb.*

A reading from the Book of Revelation   19:1, 5–9a

I, John, heard what sounded like the loud voice of a great multitude in heaven, saying:

> **"Alleluia!**
> **Salvation, glory, and might belong to our God."**

A voice coming from the throne said:

> **"Praise our God, all you his servants,**
> **and you who revere him, small and great."**

Then I heard something like the sound of a great multitude or the sound of rushing water or mighty peals of thunder, as they said:

> **"Alleluia!**
> **The Lord has established his reign,**
> **our God, the almighty.**
> **Let us rejoice and be glad**
> **and give him glory.**
> **For the wedding day of the Lamb has come,**
> **his bride has made herself ready.**

> **She was allowed to wear**
> **a bright, clean linen garment.”**

(The linen represents the righteous deeds of the holy ones.)

Then the angel said to me, “Write this: Blessed are those who have been called to the wedding feast of the Lamb.”

The word of the Lord.

Commentary

The lamb is the symbol of Jesus in the Book of Revelation. This passage is a hopeful and faith-filled look into the future of our world when it will be transformed into a kingdom of peace and justice. It is a song of joy at the nuptials between Christ and his bride, the Church, at the end of time. Marriage can be and ought to be a foretaste, for the couple and for those who are touched by them, of that special time of union and peace. That is its prophetic character. Not only is marriage, therefore, a symbol of the mystical union now existing between Christ and his Church, but it points to the final union between the Messiah and the redeemed. Some commentators attribute the custom of the bride wearing white to the white clothing of the saints who appear in the Book of Revelation.

OPTIONS FOR THE GOSPEL

G-1: Matthew 5:1–12a

1. *Rejoice and be glad, for your reward will be great in heaven.*

+ A reading from the holy Gospel according to Matthew   5:1–12a

When Jesus saw the crowds, he went up the mountain, and after he had sat down, his disciples came to him. He began to teach them, saying:

> **“Blessed are the poor in spirit,**
> **for theirs is the Kingdom of heaven.**
> **Blessed are they who mourn,**
> **for they will be comforted.**
> **Blessed are the meek,**
> **for they will inherit the land.**
> **Blessed are they who hunger and thirst for righteousness,**
> **for they will be satisfied.**
> **Blessed are the merciful,**
> **for they will be shown mercy.**
> **Blessed are the clean of heart,**
> **for they will see God.**

> **Blessed are the peacemakers,**
> **for they will be called children of God.**
> **Blessed are they who are persecuted for the sake of righteousness,**
> **for theirs is the Kingdom of heaven.**
> **Blessed are you when they insult you and persecute you**
> **and utter every kind of evil against you falsely because of me.**
> **Rejoice and be glad,**
> **for your reward will be great in heaven.”**

The Gospel of the Lord.

Commentary

In the Gospel according to Matthew, the sermon containing the Beatitudes is situated on a mountain, suggestive of Mount Sinai. The sermon is seen as the new law corresponding to the old law given to Moses. It spells out how a Christian should live in order to have joy and it is most appropriate advice for a married couple. It is not the self-satisfied, materialistic people who will be blessed and happy, but it is those who show mercy, who treat others gently, who endeavor to make peace, who are unencumbered in spirit and free to be loving who will be happy. Strengthening these habits within the marriage relationship enables partners to radiate a Christian presence beyond their home. Those who are willing to pay the price that love of and commitment to another entails will be rewarded.

G-2: Matthew 5:13–16

2. *You are the light of the world.*

+ A reading from the holy Gospel according to Matthew   5:13–16

Jesus said to his disciples: “You are the salt of the earth. But if salt loses its taste, with what can it be seasoned? It is no longer good for anything but to be thrown out and trampled underfoot. You are the light of the world. A city set on a mountain cannot be hidden. Nor do they light a lamp and then put it under a bushel basket; it is set on a lamp stand, where it gives light to all in the house. Just so, your light must shine before others, that they may see your good deeds and glorify your heavenly Father.”

The Gospel of the Lord.

Commentary

Jesus describes the nucleus of the future church as the salt of the earth, a city on a hill and a light to the world. On your wedding day, you are clearly the center of attention, the city, the light that brightens the day and the salt that gives it flavor. You are called by God to continue to be salt, light and a beacon for others. That is achieved only by loving as Jesus loved us. The quality of a bride and groom can be felt on their wedding day by the way they are concerned for others, even on that special day honoring them. It is a good time to try to live that selfless love that will continue to make you a light for others throughout your life.

G-3: Matthew 7:21, 24–29

3. LONG FORM

A wise man built his house on rock.

+ A reading from the holy Gospel according to Matthew   7:21, 24–29

Jesus said to his disciples: "Not everyone who says to me, 'Lord, Lord,' will enter the Kingdom of heaven, but only the one who does the will of my Father in heaven.

"Everyone who listens to these words of mine and acts on them will be like a wise man who built his house on rock. The rain fell, the floods came, and the winds blew and buffeted the house. But it did not collapse; it had been set solidly on rock. And everyone who listens to these words of mine but does not act on them will be like a fool who built his house on sand. The rain fell, the floods came, and the winds blew and buffeted the house. And it collapsed and was completely ruined."

When Jesus finished these words, the crowds were astonished at his teaching, for he taught them as one having authority, and not as their scribes.

The Gospel of the Lord.

OR

SHORT FORM

A wise man built his house on rock.

+ A reading from the holy Gospel according to Matthew   7:21, 24–25

Jesus said to his disciples: "Not everyone who says to me, 'Lord, Lord,' will enter the Kingdom of heaven, but only the one who does the will of my Father in heaven.

"Everyone who listens to these words of mine and acts on them will be like a wise man who built his house on rock. The rain fell, the floods came, and the winds blew and buffeted the house. But it did not collapse; it had been set solidly on rock."

The Gospel of the Lord.

Commentary

You are about to build a life together in Christian marriage. Vows made on your wedding day have to be fulfilled through a thousand acts of fidelity, compassion and love. Marriage cannot be build on shifting sands but must be built on the rock of Christ and his teachings if it is to last.

This part of the Sermon on the Mount was directed to certain prophets and healers who were upsetting the Church. The test of their work, it asserts, will not be their flashy achievements, but their obedience to the righteousness set forth in the sermon.

G-4: Matthew 19:3–6

4. *What God has united, man must not separate.*

+ A reading from the holy Gospel according to Matthew   19:3–6

Some Pharisees approached Jesus, and tested him, saying, "Is it lawful for a man to divorce his wife for any cause whatever?" He said in reply, "Have you not read that from the beginning the Creator *made them male and female* and said, *For this reason a man shall leave his father and mother and be joined to his wife, and the two shall become one flesh?* So they are no longer two, but one flesh. Therefore, what God has joined together, man must not separate."

The Gospel of the Lord.

Commentary

The Pharisees are trying to trap Jesus into taking sides in a dispute about the interpretations of a section of the Torah (the law) dealing with divorce. The Torah said that a man could divorce his wife for "some unseemly thing." Naturally the argument revolved around what was meant by "some unseemly thing." One side claimed it meant adultery; the other claimed it meant anything that displeased the husband. Jesus, in answer, harkens back to the original order of creation. It was Moses who permitted divorce as a concession to human weakness; Jesus, however, holds to the ideal that man and wife are joined together forever. The couple, assisted by God's grace in the sacrament of marriage, is called to be truly a foretaste of heavenly conditions—of fidelity beyond one's natural strength, of patience beyond one's own means. It is a prophetic vocation which deserves the support of friends and the Christian community.

G-5: Matthew 22:35–40

5. *This is the greatest and the first commandment.*
   The second is like it.

A reading from the holy Gospel according to Matthew   22:35–40

One of the Pharisees, a scholar of the law, tested Jesus by asking, "Teacher, which commandment in the law is the greatest?" He said to him, "You shall love the Lord, your God,

with all your heart, with all your soul, and with all your mind. This is the greatest and the first commandment. The second is like it: You shall love your neighbor as yourself. The whole law and the prophets depend on these two commandments.”

The Gospel of the Lord.

Commentary

This summary of the law is also found in an earlier Jewish work called the Testaments of the Twelve Patriarchs, but Jesus links the two commandments in a new way. Love of God without love of neighbor is a deception, and love of neighbor without love of God can turn out to be self-love. There are three loves which make up the two essential commandments: love of God with your whole being, love and esteem of yourself as a precious creation of God, and love of neighbor equal to the love you have for yourself. To love in this manner poses a severe challenge to us; our world does not reward or commend those who live for others. Self-centeredness (not the same as self-love) and “looking out for number one” seem to be rewarded. Married love can stand out like a beacon of hope in this dark world when it reaffirms the values of commitment, fidelity, generosity and compassion.

G-6: Mark 10:6–9

6. *They are no longer two, but one flesh.*

+ A reading from the holy Gospel according to Mark   10:6–9

> **Jesus said:**
> **“From the beginning of creation, *God made them male and female. For this reason a man shall leave his father and mother and be joined to his wife, and the two shall become one flesh.* So they are no longer two but one flesh. Therefore what God has joined together, no human being must separate.”**

The Gospel of the Lord.

Commentary

This is a Marcan parallel of G-4. The only difference between the two is that the Matthew setting is one of debate; the Mark setting is not. Consult the commentary on G-4.

G-7: John 2:1–11

7. *Jesus did this as the beginning of his signs in Cana in Galilee.*

+ A reading from the holy Gospel according to John 2:1–11

There was a wedding in Cana in Galilee, and the mother of Jesus was there. Jesus and his disciples were also invited to the wedding. When the wine ran short, the mother of Jesus said to him, "They have no wine." And Jesus said to her, "Woman, how does your concern affect me? My hour has not yet come." His mother said to the servers, "Do whatever he tells you." Now there were six stone water jars there for Jewish ceremonial washings, each holding twenty to thirty gallons. Jesus told them, "Fill the jars with water." So they filled them to the brim. Then he told them, "Draw some out now and take it to the headwaiter." So they took it. And when the headwaiter tasted the water that had become wine, without knowing where it came from (although the servants who had drawn the water knew), the headwaiter called the bridegroom and said to him, "Everyone serves good wine first, and then when people have drunk freely, an inferior one; but you have kept the good wine until now." Jesus did this as the beginning of his signs in Cana in Galilee and so revealed his glory, and his disciples began to believe in him.

The Gospel of the Lord.

Pronunciation notes:

Cana = KAY – nuh

Galilee = GAL – ih – lee

Commentary

This has been one of the most widely used texts in the Christian wedding liturgy since the Middle Ages. Jesus, who took upon himself our human flesh and condition, approves marriage by this gesture of compassion and love for the couple at Cana. The miracle is also a sign that God has broken into our history in a transforming way. Today, God promises to be with every couple in this sacrament of grace and power. Through the Spirit of Jesus granted to them, the clear, pure water of their lives together can be transformed into a fine wine, a cause of celebration for the Christian community.

G-8: John 15:9–12

8. *Remain in my love.*

+ A reading from the holy Gospel according to John 15:9–12

Jesus said to his disciples: "As the Father loves me, so I also love you. Remain in my love. If you keep my commandments, you will remain in my love, just as I have kept my Father's commandments and remain in his love.

"I have told you this so that my joy might be in you and your joy might be complete. This is my commandment: love one another as I love you.

The Gospel of the Lord.

G-9: John 15:12–16

9.   *This is my commandment: love one another.*

+ A reading from the holy Gospel according to John   15:12–16

Jesus said to his disciples: "This is my commandment: love one another as I love you. No one has greater love than this, to lay down one's life for one's friends. You are my friends if you do what I command you. I no longer call you slaves, because a slave does not know what his master is doing. I have called you friends, because I have told you everything I have heard from my Father. It was not you who chose me, but I who chose you and appointed you to go and bear fruit that will remain, so that whatever you ask the Father in my name he may give you."

The Gospel of the Lord.

Commentary (for G-8 and G-9)

In giving up his life for us, Jesus set us an example of how to live and love. God wants us to be joyful; the way to that joy is obedience to God's commands, chief of which is the command to love one another as Jesus has loved us. Our relationship with God is not that of servant to master, but of child to parent, a child who is called friend. We have been chosen to go forth and bear fruit. The fruit of this marriage will be the marriage itself and the love and progeny that will come from it. Pray to the Father in Jesus' name so that your fruit may endure.

G-10: John 17:20–26

10.   LONG FORM

That they may be brought to perfection as one.

+ A reading from the holy Gospel according to John   17:20–26

Jesus raised his eyes to heaven and said: "I pray not only for my disciples, but also for those who will believe in me through their word, so that they may all be one, as you, Father, are in me and I in you, that they also may be in us, that the world may believe that you sent me. And I have given them the glory you gave me, so that they may be one, as we are one, I in them and you in me, that they may be brought to perfection as one, that the world may know that you sent me, and that you loved them even as you loved me. Father, they are your gift to me. I wish that where I am they also may be with me, that they may see my glory that you gave me, because you loved me before the foundation of the world. Righteous Father, the world also does not know you, but I know you, and they know that you sent me.

I made known to them your name and I will make it known, that the love with which you loved me may be in them and I in them."

The Gospel of the Lord.

OR

SHORT FORM

That they may be brought to perfection as one.

+ A reading from the holy Gospel according to John   17:20–23

Jesus raised his eyes to heaven and said: "Holy Father, I pray not only for these, but also for those who will believe in me through their word, so that they may all be one, as you, Father, are in me and I in you, that they also may be in us, that the world may believe that you sent me. And I have given them the glory you gave me, so that they may be one, as we are one, I in them and you in me, that they may be brought to perfection as one, that the world may know that you sent me, and that you loved them even as you loved me."

The Gospel of the Lord.

Commentary

This reading is a love song by Christ to us. He wants us to be as he is with the Father, united in perfect union. The unity of Christians is to be a sign to the world that Jesus was sent by God. Marriage in a preeminent way is the sign of this love of God for the world. Christians strive for this kind of union but do it in a sinful world, conscious of our deep need for God's grace to touch us and transform us. That special grace is guaranteed to the wedding couple in the sacrament of marriage, not just on their wedding day, but throughout their lives together.

Acknowledgment: Two books were particularly helpful in the preparation of the commentaries in this chapter: *Preaching the Lectionary* by Reginald H. Fuller (Collegeville, MN: Liturgical Press, 1974, 1984, 2006) and *Commentaries on the Ritual Readings* by Robert Crotty and John Barry Ryan (Collegeville, MN: Pueblo Publishing Co., 1982).

CHAPTER FOUR

THE MUSIC FOR
THE WEDDING LITURGY

We turn our attention now to one of the most creative and beautiful elements of the wedding liturgy: the music. A well chosen program of music has the potential to draw people into a celebration and foster their participation in a way that words alone can never do. *Music in Catholic Worship* (OCP 10178), a document prepared by the United States Bishops' Committee on the Liturgy in 1972 and revised in 1982, notes the important role that music plays in the liturgy:

> Among the many signs and symbols used by the Church to celebrate its faith, music is of preeminent importance. As sacred song united to words it forms a necessary or integral part of the solemn liturgy. Yet the function of music is ministerial; it must serve and never dominate. Music should assist the assembled believers to express and share the gift of faith that is within them and to nourish and strengthen their interior commitment of faith. It should heighten

the texts so that they speak more fully and more effectively. The quality of joy and enthusiasm which music adds to community worship cannot be gained in any other way. It imparts a sense of unity to the congregation and sets the appropriate tone for a particular celebration.

In addition to expressing texts, music can also unveil a dimension of meaning and feeling, a communication of ideas and intuitions which words alone cannot yield. This dimension is integral to the human personality and to growth in faith. (Washington DC: United States Conference of Catholic Bishops, 1983, 23–24.)

Once in a while, the question is asked, "Must we have music at our wedding?" Anyone who has participated in a wedding where music has fulfilled its proper role will answer this question with a resounding "Yes, Amen!" Why? Because music is not simply a "nice touch" to the liturgy, but indeed draws the whole person into a spirit of celebration. Music invites the assembly to participate with heart and mind and spirit. This can happen through music with words as well as through instrumental music; both are usually used in the wedding liturgy. Singing by the assembly at a wedding expresses the joy and unity of the people gathered. It is an attractive and meaningful way of inviting guests to actually participate rather than remain spectators throughout the liturgy. Music at weddings is not only appropriate, it is encouraged.

THE MINISTERS OF MUSIC

The first step in planning the music for your wedding is to contact the parish music minister. The music minister brings a wealth of experience and can recommend music that is appropriate and which will foster active participation. You can get this person's name from your priest or deacon or the parish office. Sometimes the musician in charge of weddings is listed in the parish bulletin. A rule of thumb: contact the musician as soon as you have booked the church. Musicians' schedules fill up early. You do not have to select the music at this point, but get your wedding date and time on the musician's calendar.

Instrumentalists

Music at weddings can be accompanied by any combination of instruments. The most frequently used instruments for accompanying singing are organ, piano and guitar. Other instruments and ensembles, such as strings or brass, may add to the beauty of the wedding liturgy as well. The parish musician can suggest which instruments will best enhance the music that you select and recommend instrumentalists who are available and trained to play for wedding liturgies.

The Leader of Song

A leader of song, or cantor, is invaluable at weddings. The task of this person is to enable and motivate the song of the assembly. This is different from a soloist who usually *performs* for the assembly, although the roles are not mutually exclusive. A leader of song subtly and graciously helps the assembly to overcome the reluctance that many people feel about singing at weddings. He or she may also be able to sing a solo at appropriate times during the liturgy. The parish music minister can give you the names and phone numbers of leaders of song from the parish who are trained for this ministry and who are available to serve at weddings.

If you are considering asking a friend to sing for the wedding, be sure that he or she knows how to be a leader of song at Catholic worship. If not, your friend would function better and more comfortably as a soloist. The parish music minister might be able to teach your friend to be a leader of song, but it will take time and work. If you decide that your friend would be a good soloist but not a leader of song, then the parish music minister can suggest when the soloist would perform. Some appropriate places might be before the procession while the people are gathering or as parents are being seated (if they are not in the procession). He or she could sing a call to worship just before the procession begins or a song during the preparation of gifts. With some coaching from the music minister, the soloist might even be able to participate in the Responsorial Psalm. The important thing to remember is that performance by a soloist should never replace or distract from the singing of the assembly. Even with a soloist, a leader of song is strongly encouraged.

Last, but not least, the real question with "guest soloist" is whether or not they should sing at the wedding liturgy at all. You certainly don't want to hurt anyone's feelings (especially if they are related to you!), but in certain situations, it might be best for you to invite them to sing at the reception instead of the liturgy. Begin the wedding dinner with a religious song as part of the blessing before the meal. It can add special meaning to that moment.

WHAT SHALL WE SING?

The advice given at the end of Chapter One is worth reviewing as you begin to plan the music for the wedding liturgy. In church music today, there is a great variety of musical styles from which to choose. Besides classical liturgical repertoire, there are contemporary standard songs as well as popular religious songs that may be special to you but could be unfamiliar to your musician. In the latter case, try to bring along a copy of the music when you meet with the musician in order to facilitate the selection process which must take into consideration the three principles that follow. Take advantage of your musician's expertise in selecting music for this special celebration!

(1) **Appropriateness.** The music should be appropriate for worship. There are pastoral, liturgical and musical considerations which determine this. The music that is the most appropriate for weddings is the music of the assembly. Pay careful attention to the assembly when making choices.

The members of the assembly are not an audience; they are celebrators. Music in the liturgy is an expression of the assembly's prayer and praise to God for this wonderful occasion. For this reason, love songs that do not include God's love are inappropriate and better appreciated at the wedding reception which has its own special musical considerations. If you are considering certain favorite songs, the parish minister can suggest songs which are appropriate to the wedding liturgy and those which are more suited to other parts of the wedding celebration.

(2) Accessibility. Liturgy is, first of all, the public worship of the divine majesty. Because a wedding is liturgy, wedding music should allow and enable the assembly to give praise to God. It should also help the members of the assembly to thank God for bringing you two together. Therefore, music that will help the assembly participate more fully is what you must search out. With very little effort, you will be pleasantly surprised at how much music is accessible to you. The assembly will best pray and sing with music they have sung before. Look for acclamations, Psalms, hymns and songs, then, that are familiar to you and that you think your family and friends might know. If one of you is not Catholic, consider choosing some music that is common to Catholics and people from other faith traditions (e.g., "Praise God From Whom All Blessings Flow").

Contrary to what you may have heard, there is not a special collection of music that must be used for weddings. The music that you sing at Sunday Mass is often the music that is the core of the assembly's song. For a start, look in the hymnal or worship aid that your parish uses for a wealth of choices. Music has a powerful effect on the liturgy. We repeat: music for weddings involves informed pastoral, musical and liturgical judgment. Let the parish music minister help you decide what and when to sing. And remember that using all of your favorite music doesn't guarantee a better or more festive celebration; it only guarantees a longer one.

(3) Graciousness. Just as a hospitable greeter at the door of the church helps to make people feel welcome, so a gracious invitation to sing encourages participation and improves the quality of the singing. Ideally, a leader of song provides these invitations throughout the liturgy from the front of the church. If this is not possible, the priest or deacon could extend a personal invitation to the assembly to sing. A simple invitation will work wonders in terms of participation.

WHEN SHALL WE SING?

There are many possibilities for singing within the wedding liturgy.

The Gathering Song. A gathering song is a perfect way to invite the assembly to respond to the stirring moment of the procession. A song by the entire assembly here can truly be a joyful expression of praise and thanksgiving for God's love freely showered on us all and personified in the liturgy by both of you as witnesses to that love. After the greeting at the beginning of the liturgy (see "Beginning with Hospitality," page 28–29), the presiding minister or leader of song invites the assembly to sing the gathering song using these or similar words: "Let us continue our celebration by singing praise to God with our gathering song 'Hear Us Now, Our God and Father' (or whatever song you have chosen)."

The Responsorial Psalm. The first reading is followed by a very distinctive kind of song which belongs to the assembly. It is known as the Responsorial Psalm. There may be a variety of musical renditions, but the text is from that part of the Bible known as the Book of Psalms or the Psalter. Psalms are part of our Judaeo-Christian heritage. Jesus prayed the Psalms. The Psalm at this point in the liturgy is the assembly's way of acclaiming God's activity in humankind as proclaimed in the first reading. This is not a place for a favorite song or hymn. It is where the people respond in sung prayer in the words of our ancestors.

The assembly is seated during the Responsorial Psalm. The leader of song may sing the verses and lead the assembly in singing their easy antiphon or refrain (indicated by "R"). The *Rite of Marriage* offers a choice of seven Psalms. The parish music minister can recommend musical settings for these Psalms that are well known in the parish and that will express your prayerful sentiments on your wedding day.

As you look through the following Psalms, think about what dimension of God's love you see in each other and in your relationship. Psalms 33, 103 and 145 are full of praise and gratitude to God as they describe to us who God is. Psalm 33 emphasizes God kindness, while Psalm 103 focuses on God's mercy and Psalm 145 focuses on God's compassion. Psalm 148 praises God in all aspects of creation—an appropriate response following the first reading from the Book of Genesis (OT-1 on page 55). Psalms 112 and 128 make reference to those who fear the LORD. In biblical times, to fear the LORD meant to put the LORD first in all things. These wise words are certainly one way of including God in your marriage vows. Those who live near the desert will understand the references to olive plants in Psalm 128. When an olive plant is full from blooming out the top, the shoots grow out from the bottom of the plant—an image of abundance and the joys of family life. Psalm 34 speaks for itself: "We will see it through." Trust that the Lord will be there for you whenever you call upon him.

RP-1:   Psalm 33:12 and 18, 20–21, 22

R.   (5b) The earth is full of the goodness of the Lord.

Blessed the nation whose God is the LORD,
the people he has chosen for his own inheritance.
But see, the eyes of the LORD are upon those who fear him,
upon those who hope for his kindness.

R.   The earth is full of the goodness of the Lord.

Our soul waits for the LORD,
who is our help and our shield,
For in him our hearts rejoice;
in his holy name we trust.

R. The earth is full of the goodness of the Lord.

May your kindness, O LORD, be upon us
who have put our hope in you.

R. The earth is full of the goodness of the Lord.

RP-2: Psalm 34:2–3, 4–5, 6–7, 8–9

R. (2a) I will bless the Lord at all times.
or:
R. (9a) Taste and see the goodness of the Lord.

I will bless the LORD at all times;
his praise shall be ever in my mouth.
Let my soul glory in the LORD;
the lowly will hear me and be glad.

R.   I will bless the Lord at all times.
or:
R.   Taste and see the goodness of the Lord.

Glorify the LORD with me,
let us together extol his name.
I sought the LORD, and he answered me
and delivered me from all my fears.

R.   I will bless the Lord at all times.
or:
R.   Taste and see the goodness of the Lord.

Look to him that you may be radiant with joy,
and your faces may not blush with shame.
When the poor one called out, the LORD heard,
and from all his distress he saved him.

R.   I will bless the Lord at all times.
or:
R.   Taste and see the goodness of the Lord.

The angel of the LORD encamps
  around those who fear him, and delivers them.
Taste and see how good the LORD is;
  blessed the man who takes refuge in him.

R.   I will bless the Lord at all times.
or:
R.   Taste and see the goodness of the Lord.

RP–3:   Psalm 103:1–2, 8 and 13, 17–18a

R.   (8a) The Lord is kind and merciful.
or:
R.   (see 17) The Lord's kindness is everlasting to those who fear him.

Bless the LORD, O my soul;
  and all my being, bless his holy name.
Bless the LORD, O my soul,
  and forget not all his benefits.

R.   The Lord is kind and merciful.
or:
R.   The Lord's kindness is everlasting to those who fear him.

Merciful and gracious is the LORD,
  slow to anger and abounding in kindness.
As a father has compassion on his children,
  so the LORD has compassion on those who fear him.

R.   The Lord is kind and merciful.
or:
R.   The Lord's kindness is everlasting to those who fear him.

But the kindness of the LORD is from eternity
  to eternity toward those who fear him,
And his justice towards children's children
  among those who keep his covenant.

R.   The Lord is kind and merciful.
or:
R.   The Lord's kindness is everlasting to those who fear him.

RP-4: Psalm 112:1bc–2, 3–4, 5–7a, 7b–8, 9

R. (see 1) Blessed the man who greatly delights in the Lord's commands.
or:
R. Alleluia.

Blessed the man who fears the LORD,
who greatly delights in his commands.
His posterity shall be mighty upon the earth;
the upright generation shall be blessed.

R. Blessed the man who greatly delights in the Lord's commands.
or:
R. Alleluia.

Wealth and riches shall be in his house;
his generosity shall endure forever.
Light shines through the darkness for the upright;
he is gracious and merciful and just.

R. Blessed the man who greatly delights in the Lord's commands.
or:
R. Alleluia.

Well for the man who is gracious and lends,
who conducts his affairs with justice;
He shall never be moved;
the just one shall be in everlasting remembrance.
An evil report he shall not fear.

R. Blessed the man who greatly delights in the Lord's commands.
or:
R. Alleluia.

His heart is firm, trusting in the LORD.
His heart is steadfast; he shall not fear
till he looks down upon his foes.

R. Blessed the man who greatly delights in the Lord's commands.
or:
R. Alleluia.

Lavishly he gives to the poor;
his generosity shall endure forever;
his horn shall be exalted in glory.

R. Blessed the man who greatly delights in the Lord's commands.
or:
R. Alleluia.

RP-5:   Psalm 128:1–2, 3, 4–5

R. (see 1a) Blessed are those who fear the Lord.
or:
R. (4) See how the Lord blesses those who fear him.

Blessed are you who fear the LORD,
who walk in his ways!
For you shall eat the fruit of your handiwork;
blessed shall you be, and favored.

R. Blessed are those who fear the Lord.
or:
R. See how the Lord blesses those who fear him.

Your wife shall be like a fruitful vine
in the recesses of your home;
Your children like olive plants
around your table

R. Blessed are those who fear the Lord.
or:
R. See how the Lord blesses those who fear him.

Behold, thus is the man blessed
who fears the LORD.
The LORD bless you from Zion:
may you see the prosperity of Jerusalem
all the days of your life.

R. Blessed are those who fear the Lord.
or:
R. See how the Lord blesses those who fear him.

RP-6:   Psalm 145:8–9, 10 and 15, 17–18

R.   (9a) The Lord is compassionate toward all his works.

**The LORD is gracious and merciful,
    slow to anger and of great kindness.
The LORD is good to all
    and compassionate toward all his works.**

R.   The Lord is compassionate toward all his works.

**Let all your works give you thanks, O LORD,
    and let your faithful ones bless you.
The eyes of all look hopefully to you
    and you give them their food in due season.**

R.   The Lord is compassionate toward all his works.

**The LORD is just in all his ways
    and holy in all his works.
The LORD is near to all who call upon him,
    to all who call upon him in truth.**

R.   The Lord is compassionate toward all his works.

RP-7:   Psalm 148:1–2, 3–4, 9–10, 11–13a, 13c–14a

R.   (13a) Let all praise the name of the Lord.
or:
R. Alleluia.

**Alleluia.
Praise the LORD from the heavens,
    praise him in the heights;
Praise him, all you his angels,
    praise him, all you his hosts.**

R. Let all praise the name of the Lord.
or:
R. Alleluia.

Praise him, sun and moon;
> **praise him, all you shining stars.**
Praise him, you highest heavens,
> **and you waters above the heavens.**

R. Let all praise the name of the Lord.
or:
R. Alleluia.

You mountains and all you hills,
> **you fruit trees and all you cedars;**
You wild beasts and all tame animals,
> **you creeping things and winged fowl.**

R. Let all praise the name of the Lord.
or:
R. Alleluia.

Let the kings of the earth and all peoples,
> **the princes and all the judges of the earth,**
Young men too, and maidens,
> **old men and boys,**
Praise the name of the LORD,
> **for his name alone is exalted.**

R. Let all praise the name of the Lord.
or:
R. Alleluia.

His majesty is above earth and heaven,
> **and he has lifted his horn above the people.**

R. Let all praise the name of the Lord.
or:
R. Alleluia.

The Gospel Acclamation. The proclamation of the Gospel is preceded by a joyful "Alleluia" (except during Lent) that prepares the assembly to hear the Good News. If, for some unusual reason, the Gospel acclamation is not sung, it is omitted. In this case, ask your musicians to play instead an instrumental fanfare while the priest or deacon walks to the place where the Gospel will be proclaimed. If brass players have been hired for the wedding, the Gospel acclamation offers an opportune moment for them to participate again.

The Gospel acclamation may be done in several ways. The word "alleluia" simply may be sung repeatedly to a certain tune or the leader of song may sing a particular verse which is preceded and followed by the assembly's singing of the alleluia refrain. If the second option is chosen, these are the verses that are suggested in the *Rite of Marriage,* although others are possible:

1. 1 John 4:7b
    Everyone who loves is begotten of God and knows God.

2. 1 John 4:8b, 11
    God is love.
    If God loved us, we also must love one another.

3. 1 John 4:12
    If we love one another,
    God remains in us
    and his love is brought to perfection in us.

4. 1 John 4:16
    Whoever remains in love,
    remains in God and God in him.

During the season of Lent, a different refrain is used in place of the "alleluia" in the Gospel acclamation. Your music minister may suggest options for this lenten refrain.

The Marriage Rite. Your exchange of vows and rings is the focus of the marriage rite which takes place after the homily. Very little in the way of music is necessary at this time. A bit of instrumental music could be played while the wedding party moves into place. A brief musical acclamation (such as the "alleluia" refrain used at the Gospel acclamation) could be sung after the exchange of vows and after the exchange of rings, or at the conclusion of the marriage rite to praise God for what has just happened. Otherwise, no music is necessary at this time.

If the wedding is not taking place within a Mass (Form II or III), the liturgy concludes soon after the marriage rite. Before the Lord's Prayer and Final Blessing or at the dismissal, the assembly might be invited to sing a departure song of praise.

(The next six sections relate to weddings within Mass only. If your wedding will not be within Mass—that is, Form II or III—skip down to "Instrumental Music" on p. 96.)

Preparations of the Gifts. It is not necessary for the assembly to sing while the bread and wine are brought to the altar and prepared. Instrumental music or a short solo is appropriate here. Whatever music is used should not delay the liturgy. Do not limit yourselves to texts about bread, wine, wheat and grapes. Texts of joy, praise, love and thanksgiving are all most delightful here.

The Eucharistic Acclamations. There are three acclamations during the eucharistic prayer: the Holy, Holy after the Preface, the Memorial Acclamation after "Let us proclaim the mystery of faith," and the Great Amen at the end of the doxology ("Through him, with him, in him…"). The texts of these acclamations are presented in Chapter Two on pages 41–42. Selecting familiar settings for these acclamations is most important. But you need not worry. Your music minister can suggest settings that are commonly used in many parishes. He or she also may be familiar with some echo style acclamation in case you don't seem to come up with something familiar to everyone. You may also contact one of the Catholic music publishers listed in your parish hymnal or worship aid. They are usually more than happy to help you. If brass players have been hired for the wedding, they could accompany the assembly during the singing of these three acclamations.

The Sign of Peace. The sign of peace is not a receiving line. If people have greeted one another at the beginning of the liturgy, then this gesture can serve its intended purpose: to extend to each other a sign of Christ's peace. Singing is not recommended. Instrumental music may be used but is not recommended. As soon as the priest returns to his place at the altar, move to the breaking of the bread.

The Breaking of the Bread ("Lamb of God"). Once the sign of peace is finished, the priest breaks the Eucharistic Bread and places it in bowls for Communion. During the breaking of the Eucharistic Bread, the leader of song leads the assembly in singing the "Lamb of God." There are several familiar settings of this song which your music minister may suggest. Ideally, the song is repeated until the breaking of the Eucharistic Bread is finished.

Communion Song. Singing together is an essential sign of our communion with God and with each other. As people process to Communion, all join in singing an antiphon, Psalm or song. Since people will be receiving Communion, a refrain that they can sing without books or the printed order of celebration in their hands is suggested. The music here need not be reflective. The nature of these songs can reflect praise or thanksgiving, or God's love for humanity. The Psalms suggested in the *Rite of Marriage* (see Responsorial Psalm section) are quite appropriate here as well.

Post-Communion or Dismissal Song. The assembly may sing a final song of praise and rejoicing after Communion or at the dismissal. If a song is chosen for dismissal, it might be called a great hymn of thanksgiving and can be sung just before the departure of the bride and groom. When a festive instrumental recessional is used, a dismissal song is not necessary and often not used.

Once More from the Top. Finally on the topic of sung music, a reiteration of some advice from Chapter One: forms of personal expression, such as your favorite song, can be effectively used at the wedding, but maybe not necessarily at the wedding liturgy. All of the events associated with your wedding—rehearsal dinner, liturgy, reception—offer distinct yet ample opportunities for you to imprint your personalities on this celebration. There are many dimensions to your love for each other. Make your impression on all the events. The music at the wedding liturgy is an expression of your faith. It should reflect the gratitude and joy that you feel toward God for all the love showered on your life, especially on your wedding day. Use texts that include our loving Creator's part in your relationship. In the wedding liturgy, you will offer your lives to each other and to God.

You stand before the world as a sign that God lives and that God loves us. Let the music of the liturgy reflect this.

INSTRUMENTAL MUSIC

Music that is sung by the assembly is primary in the wedding liturgy as in all liturgies. It is not the only type of appropriate music, however. Instrumental music can effectively complement the sung music and help to shape a beautiful, prayerful liturgy.

The Processional. The entrance procession is an inspirational highlight for the assembly. It is a ceremonial movement that involves both bride and groom and liturgical ministers. Representative members of the assembly express their willingness to go forward with the bride and groom in continued friendship, support and love. The procession is a symbolic action of movement into a new life. This is the reason why many parishes and dioceses do not allow the composition popularly known as "Here Comes the Bride" to be played at weddings. Its very title limits the full meaning of the procession because, as we saw in Chapter Two, the bride and the groom are both expected to be in the procession. Interestingly, this piece is losing its popularity in many circles. Other selections, such as the "Trumpet Voluntary" attributed to Jeremiah Clarke, have replaced "Here Comes the Bride" as popular festal processionals.

There is an extensive repertoire of music for wedding processions. Confer with your music minister for advice. There are a number of recordings of commonly performed processionals available in stores and on the web, and most musicians are familiar with this music. The pieces are not very difficult to play and each one sounds terrific. Your parish may also have a recording of processionals that the music minister is proficient at playing. Remember: a modest selection played well will have a far better effect on the liturgy than a rigorous selection poorly performed.

The Recessional. There are also many possible selections for the recessional. The tune commonly referred to as the "traditional wedding march" was composed by Felix Mendelssohn and is actually becoming less customary than one might suspect. Its usage on popular television programs and soap operas has considerably diminished its popularity at church weddings. It is being enthusiastically replaced by the "Trumpet Tune" of Henry Purcell and several other selections.

Music during the Gathering and Seating of the Assembly ("Prelude Music"). There is one other area of instrumental music that needs attention: the gathering of the assembly. The music used here is crucial in setting the tone for the liturgy. From the time that people enter the church, the music which they hear creates an atmosphere of either sobriety or festivity in their consciousness. They may not be aware of this effect of music on them, but nevertheless, it is happening. Slow, quiet music will tend to have a meditative effect, resulting in an inward and reflective assembly. This makes spontaneity and participation more difficult to achieve. Baroque music, in contrast for example, bubbles with an energy and enthusiasm that encourages and fosters gregariousness which, in turn, invites participation.

It is not necessary for you to know the exact titles of music for the gathering rite. The style can be contemporary or classical. Your music minister has the musical resources to assist the liturgical function of gathering. If the musician is limited in his or her repertoire, simply request cheerful music as people gather in the church.

SOME FINAL NOTES ON THE MUSIC

Parish and Diocesan Guidelines. As was mentioned in the Introduction to this book, many parishes and dioceses have established guidelines for the wedding liturgy, including the music. These policies were not created to confine you or limit your creativity. Rather, they were probably the result of abuses to the liturgy that would offend most people. Those who are regularly involved in preparing and celebrating weddings have been forced, in the past, to witness and even implement some outrageous and extravagant spectacles. The priest, deacon or music minister can probably tell you of some fascinating yet painful experiences with weddings.

Fees. How much does all this cost? Fees vary, but when you consider the cost of clothing, flowers and food, the fees for the church musicians are a minimal, yet crucial, expense. Your parish music minister can tell you about specific fees. Find out when and where to leave your payment. It is most embarrassing and unprofessional for the musician to have to ask someone in the wedding party for a fee after the liturgy. Ask your music minister what is the procedure and then take care if it before the liturgy.

A Note to Parents. Hopefully, you will not be upset nor feel "left out" when parish policy requires that the bride and groom, not the parents, plan the music for the wedding liturgy. Marriage preparation is one way that the parish gets to know, invites into community and deepens the faith of the couple. The bride and groom should never be too busy to attend to the preparation of the wedding liturgy. It is more important than any of their other tasks of wedding preparation.

Last but not least. Do not delay in contacting the music minister and beginning the musical preparations for the wedding liturgy. Ideally, all the musical decisions should be finalized at least two weeks before the wedding. This will allow ample time for printing an order of celebration with the necessary musical information. It will also contribute much to your peace of mind and that of the musician.

CHAPTER FIVE

THE ENVIROMENT FOR
THE WEDDING LITURGY

The noted historian Jaroslav Pelikan once wrote, "Tradition is the living faith of the dead; traditionalism is the dead faith of the living" (*The Vindication of Tradition,* New Haven, CT: Yale Press, 1984, p. 65). This bit of wisdom deserves some consideration as you prepare the wedding liturgy. At every turn in the progression of this book, a gentle voice has raised an important question: in all your preparations, are you making sure that whatever is done at your wedding speaks an honest and full message of your love for each other and your regard for the people who will gather to celebrate and witness your marriage?

This book has also explored many of the signs, symbols, customs and rituals associated with weddings. Some of these elements help to tell the story of marriage today; others clearly are outmoded or tell a story contrary to how you and the Church view marriage. That is why it is so important to search the tradition for what gives life and meaning for today.

It is also important to discard those things which no longer express who we are as Christians in contemporary American culture. It takes an open mind and an honest heart to make these decisions. Avoid the persistent temptation to traditionalism. Avoid empty customs and theatrical rituals which express very little of your own best selves or of a Christian understanding of marriage.

The temptation to traditionalism is probably nowhere more difficult to overcome than in creating an environment for the "perfect" wedding. Simply put, in our culture a great deal of money rides on keeping certain customs intact and an engaged couple overspending. However, you know from your own experience that when you are guests in someone's home, it is not the lavishness of the surroundings or the richness of the food that makes for a memorable occasion. Rather, what matters most is the care with which all is prepared and the attention given to you as guests. Hospitality is primary.

A simple rule of thumb is that you can't make up in glitter and extra flowers what you lack in genuine hospitality and graciousness. If you are preoccupied and fussing over the "things" of your wedding to the exclusion of the people, then everyone has been badly served. Therefore, these thoughts on environment for a wedding will stress three very basic themes:

ONE: Less is more.

TWO: Hospitality is a fundamental form of loving.

THREE: Spectacles are better left to Broadway, Las Vegas or Ringling Brothers.

Some practical considerations:

(1) People create the mood or environment for a wedding. Therefore, know yourself and do only what you know you can handle gracefully. A classic but often repeated situation is that of the bride who has an unrealistic notion of how she should look on the wedding day. She imagines herself floating down the aisle in a dress with a seventeen-foot train. What usually happens is that reality collides with the dream. The bride finds herself out-maneuvered by the train. She is either tripping over it herself or it is being stepped on by others. Every movement of the bride during the liturgy demands that someone in the wedding party must fuss over the train. In the end, yards of unnecessary cloth have become the center of attention. The women in your wedding party end up being servants or ladies-in-waiting rather than the honored witnesses to the vows you are pronouncing.

(2) You are the ministers of the sacrament of marriage and the entire assembly is a witness to your exchange of vows. Where you sit and stand during the wedding liturgy should support these roles. Position yourselves in such a way that you can see and participate in all the actions of the liturgy and the assembly can see and hear your exchange of vows and rings. Position the two witnesses (the best man and maid/matron of honor) and other members of the wedding party (ushers and bridesmaids) in such a way that they can participate in the liturgy and not become a

well dressed wall between the assembly and you. Avoid the all too frequent practice in which the wedding party gets all dressed up at great personal expense only to spend the entire liturgy with their less flattering side facing the greatest number of people. Graciousness demands that we do not turn our backs to people. In any other circumstances it would be considered very rude.

Because each church is different, there is no one standard seating arrangement for the wedding party. Most parishes will have a suggested seating arrangement that they have found effective given the space and layout of the church. These four diagrams present possible arrangements that could be tailored to your church. Whatever arrangement you use, the important thing is that the two of you sit or stand next to each other and that you face the assembly during the marriage rite.

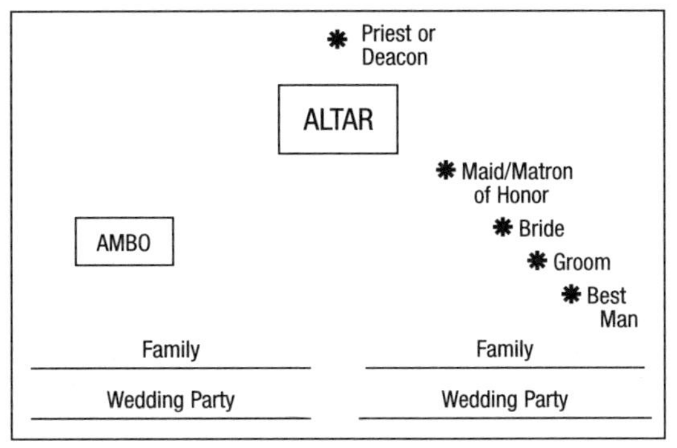

DIAGRAM A

Diagram A: The two of you and the two witnesses may be in the sanctuary throughout the entire wedding liturgy, while the other members of the wedding party sit in the second row of the assembly, right behind your immediate families. (The sanctuary is the area around the altar which usually also contains the ambo and seating for the priest or deacon and altar servers.) This arrangement allows you to have eye contact with the assembly and with the priest or deacon. You could either stand at these seats or in front of the altar (diagram C) for the exchange of vows and rings.

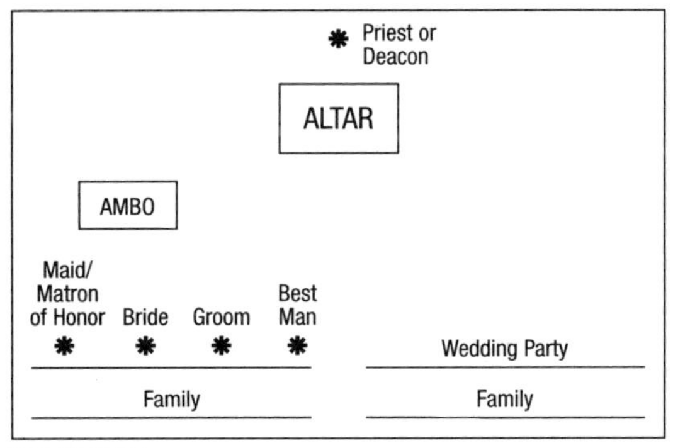

DIAGRAM B

Diagram B: The two of you and the two witnesses may sit in, or in front of, the first row of the assembly during the wedding liturgy. For the exchange of vows and rings, the four of you would come into the sanctuary and stand in front of the altar (diagram C). Other members of the wedding party and your immediate families could sit in the row behind you or in the row across the aisle.

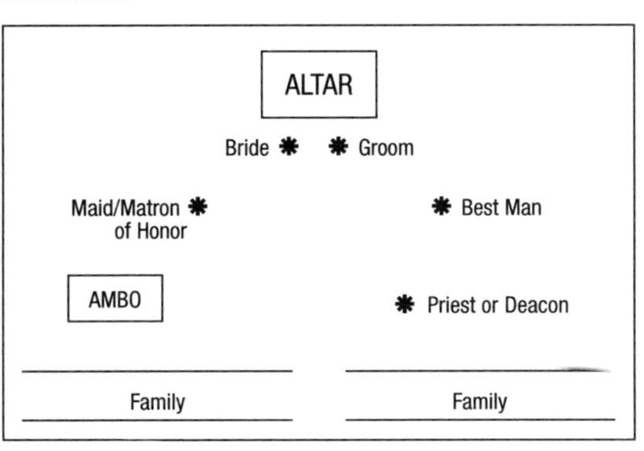

DIAGRAM C

Diagram C: An effective location for the two of you and the witnesses during the exchange of vows and rings is in front of the altar. Stand facing each other with the witnesses to your sides so that they do not obstruct the assembly's view of you. The priest or deacon stands facing you, but slightly to the side so that his back is not to the assembly. He could also stand at the head of the aisle, between the first or second row of the assembly.

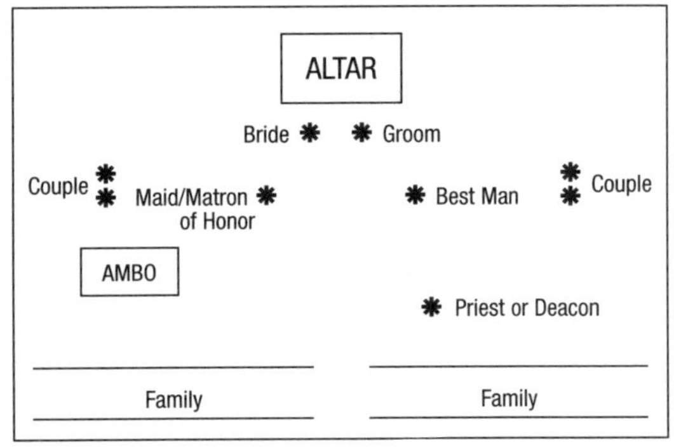

DIAGRAM D

Diagram D: In most churches, there is not enough space in the sanctuary for additional members of the wedding party. If there is enough space, however, an alternative arrangement would be to have the ushers and bridesmaids form a circle of support around the two of you as you exchange your vows and rings. Standing together as couples, the ushers and bridesmaids could take their places to the sides of the altar. The two of you and the witnesses would stand in front of the altar as in diagram C.

In some parishes, the bride and groom receive the bread and wine at the preparation of gifts from their parents, godparents or other people. The bride and groom then take the bread and wine to the altar and remain standing together as a couple near the altar until after they have received Communion. In this way, the importance of the couple as the main symbol of God's love is reinforced by their presence and visibility to the whole assembly.

(3) Furniture in the sanctuary should be limited to what is really necessary for the liturgy. If, for example, kneelers are not regularly used in your church's sanctuary, there is no reason to add them for the wedding liturgy. There are only two places in the liturgy when the assembly is directed to kneel—from the "Holy, Holy" to the "Great Amen" of the eucharistic prayer and during the breaking of the bread just before Communion—and this only pertains to weddings within Mass. There is no indication in the *Rite of Marriage* for the couple to kneel at any other time during the wedding liturgy. Excess furniture tends to visibly clutter the sanctuary and obstruct the movement of those in the sanctuary.

(4) Flowers for a wedding are usually a major expense and, yet, they are often placed in such a way that they have little visual effect or they become a real distraction or obstacle to visibility. If, for example, flowers are placed on the floor near the altar, they are often too low to be seen by the majority of the assembly, especially if the wedding party stands in front of them. In some cases, the flower arrangements are well done but placed on poorly designed stands or in locations which obstruct the movement of those in the sanctuary. Here it would be important to work with a florist who knows what is best for the particular church, rather than purchasing generic "one-size-fits-all" arrangements.

There are numerous alternatives to the customary floral arrangements seen at many weddings. Some couples simply choose to gather flowers of the season from the gardens of family and friends. Other couples put their money into flowering or green plants that can provide a beautiful setting at the wedding and then can be planted or used in their home as a reminder of the wedding. Flowers can also be used in places other than the sanctuary, particularly at the entrance or gathering space of the church, thus making a gracious sign of welcome to people as they arrive.

102

The impact of flowers at the entrance is often much greater than an arrangement lost in an already crowded sanctuary. It is a courtesy to leave the flowers at the church after the wedding for the whole parish to enjoy.

It is also important to remember that many parishes have a person or committee of people who work throughout the year at creating a worship environment which will reflect the unfolding of the various liturgical seasons. They might use banners or plants, flowers, found objects or empty spaces to express Lent, Easter, Pentecost, Advent or Christmas. These various seasonal decorations for the parish have priority over things brought in for the wedding. It is a good idea to check with the priest, deacon or wedding coordinator to see what, if any, decorations will be in place at the time of your wedding. Then, you can determine what flowers might be appropriate for the occasion. In some cases, the parish decorations are quite substantial and beautiful and you may not need any additional flowers.

Finally, if other weddings are scheduled in the church on the same day, you might consider getting together with the other couples and purchasing the flowers together. This can significantly reduce the cost for each couple. The parish can provide you with the contact information for the other couples whose weddings are scheduled for the same day.

(5) Another item that many florists offer is the aisle runner which, some historians say, originated as a cover for the dirt floors of ancient churches. Today, such an aisle runner is an unnecessary nuisance that prompts empty and often ridiculous looking ceremony for unrolling it. Most commonly, the aisle runners are made of plastic rather than cloth. When this type of runner is placed on top of carpet or highly polished stone or wood floors, a significant safety hazard is created. As people are leaving the church or going to Communion, they will have to walk on the runner. Some people could easily lose their footing or trip on the runner. (This is true even of cloth runners.) Hospitality demands consideration for those who might have difficulty walking on this surface. All in all, aisle runners are best avoided altogether.

(6) One of the consistent suggestions in this book has been to prepare and celebrate the essential elements of the Catholic wedding liturgy well, and not to let these elements be overshadowed by additional ceremonies and prayers. One such additional ceremony that you may have seen at weddings involves the lighting of a special "unity" or "marriage" candle after the exchange of vows and rings. Often, this candle is placed on the altar and surrounded by flowers. If you do decide to use this additional ceremony in the wedding liturgy, it is important to place the candle in such a way that it does not dominate the altar or distract from the importance of the Eucharist and the people in the sanctuary. A better arrangement is to place the candle on another table or stand elsewhere in the sanctuary, thus allowing the altar to serve its primary function as the table for the eucharistic meal.

(7) At important moments like a wedding, the honesty and integrity with which you present yourselves to one another, family and friends is critical. It is a time to open your hearts before God and to invite all to witness and support the sincerity of your commitment. In light of this, anything in the environment which is artificial (even silk flowers) becomes a sign contrary to what you wish to express. As the bishops of the United States said in their guidelines on art, architecture and worship, "The use of living flowers and plants, rather than artificial greens, serves as a reminder of the gift of life God has given to the human community" (*Built of Living Stones,* 129).

Above all, remember that the beauty of your wedding day and the environment for the wedding liturgy ultimately come through you, through how you choose to celebrate and express your commitment to each other, and through your gracious presence to those who have gathered to celebrate with you. Be honest, be simple, be hospitable.

PREPARING A PRINTED ORDER
OF CELEBRATION FOR THE WEDDING

A printed order of celebration—also known as a worship aid or program—is an effective way to invite the participation of all who will gather to celebrate your marriage. The order of celebration, containing the music and an outline of the wedding liturgy, need not be fancy or elaborate. A simple, well-designed order of celebration can be an attractive reminder of the wedding, while primarily serving to provide the texts and subtle directions needed by the assembly. Before printing the order of celebration, make sure that you have finalized the choices of prayers, readings and music with the priest or deacon and the music minister.

As you can see from the two sample orders of celebration on the following pages, the outline is highlighted by printing headings for the various parts of the wedding liturgy. It is unnecessary to print the text of the readings, the vows or the prayers spoken by the priest or deacon since these are intended to be heard, not read by everyone. The words and music of songs, refrains and acclamations are reprinted to enable everyone to sing. Subtle directions for when to sit and stand as well as the response to the readings and to the prayer of the faithful may be included to assist those who may be unfamiliar with the Catholic liturgy.

The parish music minister can provide you with the music and words of the songs for the order of celebration. He or she can also help you to arrange for the necessary permission to reprint the music in your order of celebration. Reprinting music, including the music that appears in the sample orders of celebration on the following pages or even just the words of a song, without the permission of the publisher is a violation of United States copyright law. The benefit of having the music easily accessible to the assembly will be well worth the one or two phone calls or letters that may be required to obtain reprint permission. In many cases, the parish may have a license that allows reprinting of music from a particular publisher for all liturgies in the parish. A simple acknowledgment of the copyright should be printed under each song or at the end of the order of celebration.

The appearance of the order of celebration can add to the beauty of the wedding. If there is an artist among your relatives or friends, ask that person to design a cover or do the lettering in calligraphy. Art from this book may also be reproduced in your order of celebration. An effective size of paper for the order of celebration is 8½" x 14", folded in half to make an 8½" x 7" booklet. Attractive paper is available at many printers and office supply stores; take the time to shop around for the best selection and price.

The two sample orders of celebration that follow are provided as models for your own order of celebration. The first is for a wedding within Mass (Form I) and the second is for a wedding outside of Mass (Form II or III). In the second sample, the assembly is being invited to join the priest in the blessing of the couple, a suggestion discussed on page 51. This may be done at any wedding, whether Mass is celebrated or not. You might also ask the parish music minister for orders of celebration from previous weddings to use as models. Some parishes provide the order of celebration for weddings, so be sure to check with the wedding coordinator or music minister first.

Holy Angels Parish
celebrates the wedding of
Sarah Ann Johnson
and
Don Howard Giannella

Saturday, June 25

Welcome to our family members and friends who have gathered to celebrate our marriage today. We thank each of you for coming from near or far to be with us as we begin our married life.

This program contains the music and an outline of the service for our wedding celebration. We invite you to sing and participate fully! We also kindly ask that flash photography not be used during the wedding.

Sarah and Don

* * * * *

INTRODUCTORY RITES

Gathering Music/Prelude

Procession (stand):   "Trumpet Tune" (H. Purcell)

Gathering Song: "Hear Us Now, Our God and Father" (HYFRYDOL)

Text: 87 87 D; Vss. 1–2, Harry N. Huxhold, © 1978, Lutheran Book of Worship. All rights reserved.
Used with permission of Augsburg Fortress. Vs. 3, John Newton, 1725–1807, alt. Music: Rowland H. Prichard, 1811–1887.

Opening Prayer

LITURGY OF THE WORD

First Reading (sit):	Genesis 1:26–28, 31a
Response:	**Thanks be to God.**
Responsorial Psalm:	"Blessed Are Those Who Fear the Lord" (Psalm 128; O. Alstott)

Music: Owen Alstott, © 1977, 1990, OCP. All rights reserved.
Text: © 1969, 1981, 1997, International Committee on English in the Liturgy, Inc. (ICEL).

Second Reading:	Colossians 3:12–17
Response:	**Thanks be to God.**
Gospel Acclamation (stand):	"Celtic Alleluia" (F. O'Carroll/C. Walker)

© 1985, 1996, Fintan O'Carroll and Christopher Walker.
Published by OCP. All rights reserved.

Gospel:	Matthew 5:13–16
Response:	**Praise to you, Lord Jesus Christ.**
Homily (sit)	

RITE OF MARRIAGE

Statement of Intentions

Consent and Exchange of Vows

    Acclamation: "Celtic Alleluia" (above)

Blessing and Exchange of Rings

    Acclamation: "Celtic Alleluia" (above)

Prayer of the Faithful

    Response: **Lord, hear our prayer.**

LITURGY OF THE EUCHARIST

Preparation of the Altar and Gifts

Eucharistic Prayer: (*Heritage Mass* acclamations; O. Alstott)

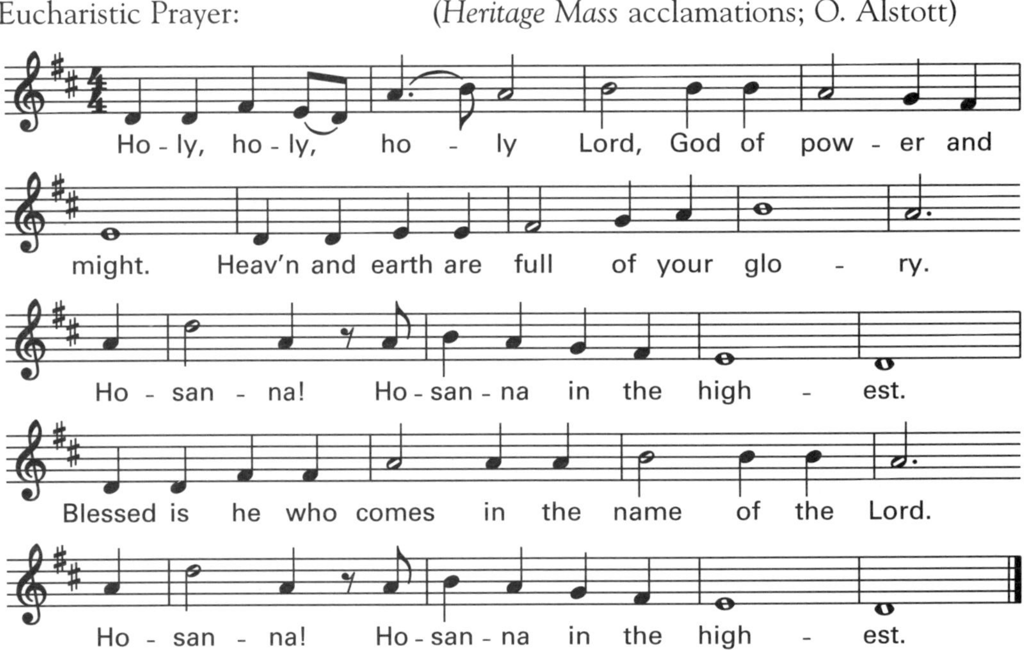

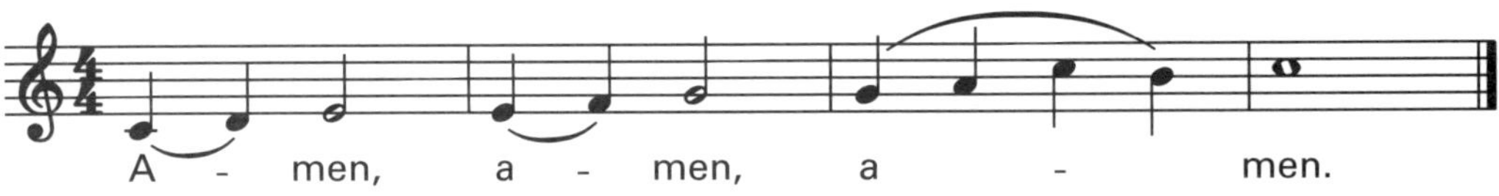

The Lord's Prayer (stand)

The Nuptial Blessing

Sign of Peace

Breaking of the Bread: "Lamb of God" (*Heritage Mass;* O. Alstott)

Communion: "Christ, Be Our Light" (B. Farrell)

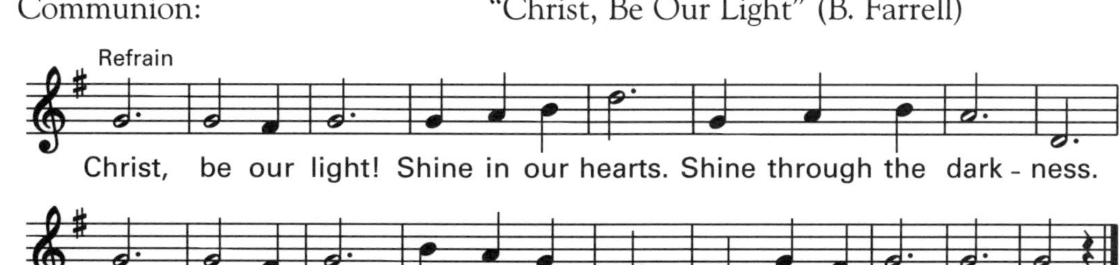

CONCLUDING RITES

Final Blessing (stand)

Recessional: "Trumpet Voluntary" (J. Clarke)

THE WEDDING PARTY

Amy Tozler, maid of honor

Brian Giannella, best man

Brenda Johnson and Paul Torres

Susan Cohen and James Haley

MINISTERS OF THE LITURGY

Father James Thompson, presiding minister

Roxie MacFarlan, cantor

Anne McAndrew, Suzie Russell and Steve Morics, ministers of music

Joe Niegoski and Ann McDonald, readers

Grace Johnson and John Panetti, gift bearers

Mary Frances Sosa and Philip and Celestine Jones,
extraordinary ministers of holy Communion

Saint Patrick Parish
celebrates the wedding of
Arthur Sean Moore
and
Maria Kathleen O'Connor

Saturday, October 24

As we gather to celebrate our wedding, we want to thank each of you who has joined us from near and far. You have each been an important part of our lives and we thank you for the support you have given us during our engagement.

We have enjoyed preparing this wedding liturgy with Father Broderick and Reverend Ferguson. Please join in singing the music that is printed in this program. Welcome!

Arthur and Maria

INTRODUCTORY RITES

Gathering Music/Prelude

Procession (stand): "Love Divine, All Loves Excelling" (HYFRYDOL)

Text: 87 87 D; Charles Wesley, 1707–1788, alt. Music: Rowland H. Prichard, 1811–1887.

Opening Prayer

LITURGY OF THE WORD

First Reading (sit):	Song of Songs 2:8–10, 14, 16a; 8:6–7a
Response:	**Thanks be to God.**
Responsorial Psalm:	"Taste and See" (Psalm 34; J. Schiavone)

Second Reading:	1 Corinthians 12:31—13:8a
Response:	**Thanks be to God.**
Gospel Acclamation (stand):	"Celtic Alleluia" (F. O'Carroll/C. Walker)

Gospel:	John 15:9–12
Response:	**Praise to you, Lord Jesus Christ**
Homily (sit)	

RITE OF MARRIAGE

Statement of Intentions

Consent and Exchange of Vows

Acclamation:	"Celtic Alleluia" (above)

Blessing and Exchange of Rings

Acclamation:	"Celtic Alleluia" (above)

Prayer of the Faithful

Response:	**Lord, hear our prayer.**

The Nuptial Blessing

CONCLUDING RITES

The Lord's Prayer   **Our Father, who art in heaven,
hallowed be thy name;
thy kingdom come;
thy will be done on earth as it is in heaven.
Give us this day our daily bread;
and forgive us our trespasses
as we forgive those who trespass against us;
and lead us not into temptation,
but deliver us from evil.
For thine is the kingdom, and the power,
and the glory, for ever and ever. Amen.**

Final Blessing
(Please join in this blessing by extending your arms toward
Arthur and Maria as Father Broderick proclaims the blessing prayer.)

Recessional: "Rondeau" (J. Mouret)

* * * * *

THE WEDDING PARTY

George Perez, best man

Jane O'Brien, maid of honor

Kurt Baker and Hillary Brown

Justin Wentworth and Marilyn Heintschel

MINISTERS OF THE LITURGY

Reverend Michael Broderick, Saint Patrick Church

Reverend Barbara Ferguson, Christ Episcopal Church

Andrea Goodrich, cantor

Jane O'Keefe, Joe Ganley and Michael Gribshaw, ministers of music

Tran Khac Hy and Teresa O'Brien, readers

WEDDING MUSIC REPERTOIRE

Some additional music suggestions (including traditional hymns with alternative texts for weddings):

Gathering / Opening Hymns & Songs (after the Instrumental Processional)
All Creatures of Our God and King (LASST UNS ERFREUEN)
All People That on Earth Do Dwell (OLD HUNDREDTH)
For the Beauty of the Earth (DIX)
God, Who Created Hearts to Love (Ridge)
Hear Us Now, Our God and Father (HYFRYDOL)
Love Divine, All Loves Excelling (HYFRYDOL)
Love Is the Sunlight (BUNESSAN)
Morning Has Broken (BUNESSAN)
O Come, All Ye Faithful (during Christmas Season)
Praise God from Whom All Blessings Flow (OLD HUNDREDTH)
Table of Plenty (Schutte)
This Day God Gives Me (BUNESSAN)

Preparation of the Gifts
Come, My Way, My Truth, My Life (THE CALL/Vaughan Williams)
Prayer of St. Francis (Temple)
The Lord Is My Light (Walker)
To Believe in Love (Whitaker)
You Alone (Hart)

Communion
Be Not Afraid (Dufford)
How Great Thou Art (Hine)
Love Which Never Ends (Sands)
May Love Be Ours (Schutte)
My Soul Rejoices (Alstott)
One Bread, One Body (Foley)
Our Blessing Cup (Hurd)
Somos el Cuerpo de Cristo/We Are the Body of Christ (Cortez)
Ubi Caritas (Hurd)
Ven al Banquete/Come to the Feast (Hurd/Moriarty)
Where Love is Found (Schutte)
Wherever You Go (Norbet/Weston Priory)

SAMPLE PRAYERS OF THE FAITHFUL

Sample Prayer of the Faithful #1

Priest or Deacon: Filled with the joy of this celebration, we bring before God our prayers for *N.* and *N.*, for the Church and for the world.

Reader: For the Church throughout the world and for the parishes of which *N.* and *N.* have been a part; (here name the churches where you were baptized, where you celebrated first Communion and confirmation, and other parishes or college chapel communities of which you have been a part), let us pray to the Lord:

All: **Lord, hear our prayer.**

Reader: For our nation and this city/town, and for those who serve in our government, let us pray to the Lord:

All: **Lord, hear our prayer.**

Reader: For the poor, the homeless and the unemployed, and for all who suffer under persecution, let us pray to the Lord:

All: **Lord, hear our prayer.**

Reader: For *N.* and *N.* and all married couples, for their faithfulness to each other and for their loving service of the Gospel, let us pray to the Lord:

All: **Lord, hear our prayer.**

Reader: For the parents and families of *N.* and *N.*, for their godparents (here name your godparents), and for all who formed them in faith, let us pray to the Lord:

All: **Lord, hear our prayer.**

Reader: For the deceased relatives of *N.* and *N.*, for the sick and for those unable to be with us today, let us pray to the Lord:

All: **Lord, hear our prayer.**

Priest or Deacon: Gracious God, your Son, our Lord Jesus Christ, poured forth blessings on the wedding couple at Cana. Look with kindness on *N.* and *N.* as they pledge their lives to one another in the presence of your Church. May they cherish one another and be heartened by your love. Through them, may your Church be blessed. We ask this through Christ our Lord.

All: **Amen.**

Sample Prayer of the Faithful #2

Priest or Deacon: Gathered in joyful hope, we offer our prayers to God, who creates hearts to love.

Reader: For the Church and those who serve the Church and for all people who preach and practice the Gospel of Christ, we pray to the Lord:

All: Lord, hear our prayer.

Reader: For the Jewish people, the first to hear the Word of God, and for their continual growth in the love of God's name and in faithfulness to the covenant, we pray to the Lord:

All: Lord, hear our prayer.

Reader: For the outcasts and downtrodden of our city/town and our nation, and for churches and families who offer them refuge and compassion, we pray to the Lord:

All: Lord, hear our prayer.

Reader: For the Lord's abundant blessings on *N.* and *N.* in their married life, we pray to the Lord:

All: Lord, hear our prayer.

Reader: For the families and friends of *N.* and *N.* gathered here today and for our support of one another in times of need as we rejoice with one another today, we pray to the Lord:

All: Lord, hear our prayer.

Reader: For family members who have gone before us marked with the sign of faith: (here name deceased relatives), we pray to the Lord:

All: Lord, hear our prayer.

Priest or Deacon: God our Creator, guardian of our homes and source of all blessings, you delight in the happiness of your people. Hear the prayers this Church offers for *N.* and *N.*, for all your people and for all the world. Fulfill our needs and guide our actions toward the building up of your kingdom. We ask this through Christ our Lord.

All: Amen.

BLESSINGS RELATED TO THE PERIOD OF ENGAGEMENT

The Church has a wonderful tradition of blessing people at key moments in their lives. As you prepare for the wedding liturgy and for married life, you might consider celebrating one or both of the following blessing with your families. They are taken from *Catholic Household Blessings and Prayers*, a prayerbook published by the United States Catholic Bishops' Committee on the Liturgy. This prayerbook is a handsome resource for developing a tradition of family prayer in your home.

Blessing of an Engaged Couple

Ordinarily, the blessing of an engaged couple is celebrated by both families, perhaps at a meal together.

All make the Sign of the Cross. One of the parents begins:

Brothers and sisters,
let us praise our Lord Jesus Christ,
who loved us and gave himself for us.
Let us bless him now and for ever.

All respond:

Blessed be God for ever.

The leader may use these or similar words to introduce the blessing;

We know that all of us need God's blessings at all times; but at the time of their engagement to be married, Christians are in particular need of grace as they prepare themselves to form a new family. Let us pray, then, for God's blessings to come upon this couple, our brother and sister: that as they await the day of their wedding, they will grow in mutual respect and in their love for one another; that through their companionship and prayer together they will prepare themselves rightly and chastely for marriage.

Then the Scripture is read:

Listen to the words of the apostle Paul to the Corinthians:

> Love is patient, love is kind. It is not jealous, [love] is not pompous, it is not
> inflated, it is not rude, it does not seek its own interests, it is not quick-tempered,

it does not brood over injury, it does not rejoice over wrongdoing but rejoices with the truth. It bears all things, believes all things, hopes all things, endures all things.

Love never fails. If there are prophecies, they will be brought to nothing; if tongues, they will cease; if knowledge, it will be brought to nothing. For we know partially and we prophesy partially, but when the perfect comes, the partial will pass away. When I was a child, I used to talk as a child, think as a child, reason as a child; when I became a man, I put aside childish things. At the present we see indistinctly, as in a mirror, but then face to face. At present I know partially; then I shall know fully, as I am fully known. So faith, hope, love remain, these three; but the greatest of these is love.

1 Corinthians 13:4–13 (New American Bible)

(The family's Bible may be used for an alternative reading such as John 15:9–12.)

The reader concludes:

The Word of the Lord.

All respond:

Thanks be to God.

After a time of silence, all join in prayers of intercession for the couple and for others. All recite the Lord's Prayer. Then the engaged couple may exchange rings or some other gift that signifies their pledge to each other. One of the parents may bless these gifts:

N. and *N.,* in due course may you honor the sacred pledge symbolized by these gifts which you now exchange.

R. Amen.

Parents may then place their hands on their children's heads in blessing. One or more of the parents speaks the blessing:

We praise you, Lord,
for your gentle plan draws together
your children, *N.* and *N.,*
in love for one another.
Strengthen their hearts,
so that they will keep faith with each other,
please you in all things,
and so come to the happiness of celebrating
the sacrament of their marriage.

We ask this through Christ our Lord.

R. Amen.

May the God of love and peace
abide in you, guide your steps,
and confirm your hearts in his love,
now and for ever.

R. Amen.

The blessing may conclude with song. The following may be sung to a tune such as OLD HUNDREDTH ("Praise God from Whom All Blessings Flow").

From all that dwell below the skies,
    Let the Creator's praise arise;
Let the Redeemer's name be sung,
    Through ev'ry land by ev'ry tongue.

In ev'ry land begin the song;
    To ev'ry land the strains belong;
In cheerful sounds all voices raise,
    And fill the world with loudest praise.

(Text based on Psalm 117; Vs. 1: Isaac Watts, 1674–1748; Vs. 2, anonymous.)

Blessing of a Son or Daughter Before Marriage

Before the wedding, the family may gather around its member who is to be married, perhaps at a special meal in the family's home.

All make the Sign of the Cross. A parent begins:

Let us bless the Lord,
by whose goodness we live
and by whose grace we love one another.
Blessed be God for ever.

All respond:

Blessed be God for ever.

Then the Scripture is read:

Listen to the word of the book of Deuteronomy:

> Hear, O Israel! The LORD is our God, the LORD alone! Therefore, you shall love the LORD, your God, with all your heart, and with all your soul, and with all your strength. Take to heart these words which I enjoin on you today. Drill them into your children. Speak of them at home and abroad, whether you are busy or at rest.

> Deuteronomy 6:4–7 *(New American Bible)*

The reader concludes:

The Word of the Lord.

All respond:

Thanks be to God.

The parents may give a Bible to the one who is to be married. Then all join in prayers of intercession for the couple to be married and for the world. After the Lord's Prayer, the parents and other family members place their hands on the head of their son/daughter as one parent speaks the blessing.

May the Lord, who gave you into our care
and made you a joy to our home,
bless you and keep you.

R. Amen.

May the Lord, who turns the hearts of parents to their children
and the hearts of children to their parents,
smile on you and be kind to you.

R. Amen.

May the Lord, who delights in our love for one another,
turn toward you and give you peace.

R. Amen.

All make the Sign of the Cross as the leader concludes:

May the God of love and peace
abide in you, guide your steps,
and confirm your hearts in his love,
now and for ever.

R. Amen.

A FAMILY CELEBRATION OF LEAVE-TAKING

The two blessings on the previous pages can help you and your families celebrate your transition into married life. Families have also developed their own rituals which acknowledge and ease the change that takes place when one leaves home to get married. Sister of St. Joseph of Chestnut Hill Dolores Clerico, the Director of the Office of Lay Leadership for the Diocese of Camden, New Jersey, encourages engaged couples to incorporate family celebrations of "leave-taking" into their time of preparation for marriage:

Your wedding marks a major transition in life. In moving from single to married life, each of you leaves a particular place within the original family in order to vow lifetime commitment to a new family. Relational ties with your families are not severed, but they *are* changed.

The process of separating from home occurs over a period of time, as does the process of becoming married. Neither happens with one walk down the aisle! Perhaps you moved from your family home long ago; maybe you are just now moving from there. In either case, the impact of your familial relationships will extend throughout your life and will influence new relationships, especially the one you will share as a married couple. No doubt you have spent time discussing this in preparing for marriage.

It is important to realize that the transition through which you are presently moving affects not just the two of you, but each of your families as well. The commitment you are making to one another will give a new and different shape to the way you, your parents and your siblings relate to one another. This normal transition in life often brings to the surface a wide range of feelings for everyone.

In the preceding chapters of this book, you have seen how the wedding liturgy publicly ritualizes the profound nature of your relationship and the future you willingly embrace together. Before this wedding ritual takes place, we encourage you to plan a "leave-taking" event within each of your families. Such a ritual can allow each family to recall its common history, to name the shift that is now taking place in the family and to acknowledge the emotions that are present for all involved. A leave-taking ritual is a way for the members of each family to support one another in this new phase of family life. It is an opportunity for celebrating as well as for letting-go and healing where this is needed.

What would a leave-taking ritual look like? One possibility is to gather your parents and siblings together for a simple meal. During your time together, invite the sharing of stories and memories; recall how you have celebrated holidays and significant life events. Share how each one has influenced the other. Don't be afraid to acknowledge failure or the need to forgive! Mention a married couple from the family tree that is admired and why. Express what you wish for one another. Perhaps your parents could pass on a special tradition or family heirloom to you. Together thank God for what you have shared over the years and ask God's blessing on your original family as well as your future family.

The above suggestions are meant to stimulate your own ideas. Depending upon circumstances, you may or may not choose to be present as a couple for both leave-taking rituals. If you decide to be present for each family's gathering, be sure to include welcoming your partner into the family and ask for your family's love and support as you shift your primary loyalty from them to your future spouse.

Because your wedding signals the end of an era as well as the beginning of an era, it can be a bitter-sweet experience for you and your families. As with all major life transitions, it may engender both excitement and apprehension. At this sacred yet ordinary moment when God touches you to the core, a family leave-taking ritual can speak to all these feelings.

CELEBRATING A CATHOLIC WEDDING
IF YOU WERE MARRIED OUTSIDE
THE CATHOLIC CHURCH
(CONVALIDATION)

The Church welcomes couples who were married outside the Catholic Church and who now wish to have their marriage recognized as valid in the Catholic Church. Priests, deacons and other parish ministers, working with the staff at the Tribunal in your local diocese, will guide and accompany you through the process leading up to the celebration of your marriage in the Catholic Church. Much of the information in this book will apply to the celebration of your wedding. The following two essays provide additional information and background that may be helpful as you prepare. The first is by Linda Weigel, the Director of the Tribunal and Canonical Services in the Archdiocese of Portland in Oregon. The second is by Father Daniel Adams, the Pastor of Saint Cyril Parish in Wilsonville, Oregon.

A Canon Lawyer's Perspective on Convalidation

At times, couples preparing for marriage may presently be in a civil marriage, and now wish to validate their union in the Catholic Church. It may be that you were married in a civil ceremony for any number of reasons, and because one or both of you are Catholic, you now wish to have your union recognized as valid in the Catholic Church. If this describes your situation, you may find it helpful to consider some pastoral, canonical and liturgical insights as you begin your planning with a priest, deacon or other pastoral minister who is assisting you in your preparations.

Seeking Convalidation

Although some situations requiring convalidation might involve different or complicated scenarios, the great majority of couples who need to validate their marriage will seek a convalidation; that is, a **new celebration of the marriage consent** in a public manner in the Catholic Church. In other words, you are seeking to express your vows in the Catholic marriage rite. For example, you might be in a civil marriage and now you wish to make that union one that is recognized as valid by the Catholic Church. Or, one of both of you may have been previously married and have not been free to marry. Then, if you have had that former marriage studied by the ecclesiastical Tribunal and have received a declaration of invalidity and freedom to marry, you may now wish to convalidate that earlier civil union by means of giving consent in the rite of marriage.

The Tribunal

You will want to be sure that you do not schedule a convalidation before completing any needed annulment process through the Church courts known as the Tribunal. When the study of your former marriage is complete and you receive an affirmative decision from the Tribunal, you will receive a Declaration of Invalidity and freedom to marry. At times, there may be a restriction placed, asking that issues be addressed before another marriage takes place. The restriction may be noted as a *Vetitum* or *Monitum.* You might think of the *Vetitum* as a flashing red light, and the *Monitum* as a flashing yellow light, indicating caution before proceeding. Often, what is asked is that the person address certain concerns that caused upset in the former marriage, such as addiction or anger issues. Other areas that might need discussion and counseling are areas of loss or grief, such that could negatively impact a future marriage. If you can look upon any restriction as a help and a guide to assist you in forming a healthy new marital partnership, it will be worth the effort you give in attending to your readiness and growth.

A Healthy Marriage

Sometimes a couple finds that their civil marriage is undergoing great difficulty and may no longer even seem viable. The outlook for a loving and mutual marriage may not appear very strong to one or even to both parties. At those times, you might envision that convalidating your civil marriage and having it recognized as valid in the Catholic Church will bring a needed element to the marriage to "make" it healthy. While this is understandable, it can be a mistake to convalidate an unhealthy and unloving marriage simply as a "last ditch" effort to make the marriage right. Unfortunately, in these situations, your marriage will not automatically become a healthy partnership without some work. What is first needed will be effort spent with a skilled pastoral counselor to work on issues such as communication and honesty within the marriage to bring healing and health into the marital partnership.

A New Consent

Simply put, all persons who are Catholic by baptism or by formal reception into the Catholic Church are required to marry according to Catholic "form" of marriage. That form is present when the parties exchange their marriage consent in the presence of an official Catholic witness, such as a delegated priest or deacon, and two other witnesses who are able to attest to the fact that the marriage took place. Sometimes, for certain reasons, a priest might request a **dispensation from form of marriage** for a couple. For instance, if the one of the parties is a member of another faith and if both parties understand that the Catholic party will maintain his or her Catholic faith and do all that can be done to raise any children in the Catholic faith, then it might be permitted that the couple marry in the church of the non-Catholic person, with a dispensation. This is but one example of some reasons for this request. However, if a Catholic enters a civil marriage only, and no dispensation has been given, that is when convalidation later comes into the picture. In your preparation for convalidation, you will discuss the fact that your civil marriage is not considered a valid one in the Catholic church and so a new consent must be given. In other words, you are newly consenting to this marriage now taking place in the Catholic Church. This convalidation is not a blessing of your civil marriage. It is a new consent that brings something new into being—the bond of marriage. Your preparation at the parish will assist you in developing a deeper understanding of this concept.

A Pastor's Perspective on Convalidation

Two common misconceptions exist when a couple approaches the Church for the convalidation of their marriage: either that they know everything about marriage, or that they know nothing. Bearing this in mind, if you are coming forward for convalidation, you have every right to expect that your experience as a married couple will be respected. You have already negotiated what it means to transition from a single life style into a married one; you likely have identified in very practical ways both your strengths and weaknesses in communication; and you have discussed with each other your reasons for coming to the Church to ask for convalidation. At the same time, there is something substantially new occurring as you enter into marriage within the Church, and a different standard will be applied to your relationship. More than committing to a civil contract, you are now asked to embody the reality of God's love in the world. Clearly through this convalidation a new reality is coming to pass.

What does this new reality look like? From the perspective of the Church, your marriage will certainly proclaim a unity between the two of you. But it will also be understood to be an encounter with God's love. Put simply, it means that when you want to see God's love embodied, you look first to your spouse. When you want to know God's pardon, you reflect on your experiences of forgiveness in your marriage. When you need either God's comfort or motivation, you turn towards one another. The *divine* love is to become visible through *your* love. Moreover the blessings of your relationship as husband and wife are not meant only for you, but for the benefit of the larger community as well. Your proclamation of vows in the context of the Church signals your intention to offer this love, forgiveness, comfort and motivation to those who surround you.

Embracing this view of marriage requires adequate reflection, and a period of preparation is provided by your local parish as you ready yourselves for the sacrament. The same is true of any couple wanting to be married in the Church. This preparation will take into account your lived experience while exploring the deeper meaning of what you're about to do. Issues such as spirituality, religious practices and how your children will be raised in the faith will be at the center of the discussion. Matters that you're already well acquainted with—finances, in-laws, sexuality, roles in marriage, conflict resolution—will also be considered, but now through the lens of what it means to be married in the church.

To be active participants in the preparation, take this opportunity to reflect on the quality of your present relationship. What do you do well as a couple? In what ways do you want to grow and progress? What behaviors do you want to introduce or emphasize? What ones would you like to leave behind? While being grateful for the richness of your life together to this point, now would be the perfect time to make a new beginning as you consciously invite the grace of God to be with you in your marriage.

Diocesan regulations vary, specifying that this time of preparation happen over a period of several months prior to the wedding. In addition to the actual preparation, some documents about your baptism and additional forms will need to be assembled. If either of you has had a previous marriage, more time will be required. You would do well to contact your parish as soon as possible to make all the arrangements.

As part of the preparation, you will be making selections for the wedding ceremony. You may be wondering about the differences between your convalidation ceremony and a marriage ceremony of a couple who has not been civilly married. The short answer is "none." Though there might be an impulse to treat these as different realities, they are, in essence, the same. At times, convalidation couples might be counseled to have a quiet, simple ceremony with just a few people present since it is, in the view of some, "just a blessing." But as has been discussed previously, this moment is a new beginning and a new consent. Therefore, the size and shape of the ceremony is dictated by the new reality that's taking place. The ceremony need not be either lavish or inconsequential, but it should authentically reflect what is happening. Other chapters in this book will help you make choices in a reflective and conscious manner. In particular, if there are children from your previous union, you may want to review the suggestions on how to include them in the ritual (detailed elsewhere in this book).

But before all else, it's important that you know that your convalidation blesses the Church community. We can never have too many reminders of what the love of God looks like, and in your mutual love, we get a fuller picture of God's enduring care for us in every circumstance of our lives, "for better, for worse, for richer and for poorer, in sickness and in health."

ABOUT THE AUTHORS

Paul Covino is Associate Chaplain and Director of Liturgy at the College of the Holy Cross in Worcester, Massachusetts and adjunct faculty member for the Georgetown Center for Liturgy. He is a member of the Catholic Common Ground Initiative Committee and served on the U.S. Bishops' Committee on the Liturgy Task Group on American Adaptations of the *Order for Celebrating Marriage*. Paul has directed wedding preparation programs for engaged couples and wedding workshops for pastoral ministers throughout the United States and Canada, and has written numerous articles about the celebration of Catholic weddings and other liturgical issues. He was study guide author and consultant for the video *Our Catholic Wedding* (OCP 11520) and writes a weekly column for *Today's Liturgy* magazine and liturgy.com.

Lawrence Madden, S.J. is the director of the Georgetown Center for Liturgy which he founded in 1981 and an adjunct member of the Theology faculty at Georgetown University. He has served as advisor to the U.S. Bishops' Committee on the Liturgy, Director of Campus Ministry at Georgetown University and Pastor of Holy Trinity Catholic Church in Washington, D.C. A frequent presider and preacher at weddings, Larry has written numerous articles on liturgical topics and co-authored and edited several books including *The Joseph Campbell Phenomenon: Implications for the Contemporary Church* (OCP 6054). He has lectured widely at various diocesan and national conferences and at convocations and retreats for clergy. He earned a doctorate in theology and a diploma in liturgical studies from the University of Trier, Germany.

Elaine Rendler-McQueeney, DMA, is a musician, author, teacher and frequent workshop leader in the U.S. and Canada. An organ student of Alexander McCurdy, she earned her doctorate at The Catholic University of America under Conrad Bernier and Daniel Roth. Elaine is currently Associate Professor of music theory at George Mason University, Fairfax, Virginia. Besides her weekly column for *Today's Liturgy* magazine and liturgy.com, her books include *In the Midst of the Assembly* (OCP 9664) and *This Is the Day* (OCP 10106), and her music publications include *Keyboard Praise* (OCP 11061), *The Seven Last Words of Christ* (OCP 11381) and *Sabbath Gate: Enter with Jubilee* (OCP 10985).

John Buscemi is an artist, liturgist and teacher at Dominican University in Chicago. He is a liturgical designer with over 25 years of experience and has been part of nearly one hundred church building and renovation projects throughout the United States and Canada. His main focus is finding the intersections in people's lives where liturgy, spirituality and the arts meet. John is the author of *Places for Devotion* (Liturgy Training Publications).

* * * * *

The Georgetown Center for Liturgy, (centerforliturgy.georgetown.edu) founded in 1981 by Georgetown University and Holy Trinity Parish in Washington, D.C., is an education, research and consultation center dedicated to transforming American Catholic parishes through the liturgical renewal initiated by the Second Vatican Council.